Lloyd Photo.] Southport.
J. RICKERBY, Esq., SOUTHPORT.
Originator of the Volume and Supporter of A. R. Downer

RUNNING RECOLLECTIONS

AND HOW TO TRAIN.

Being an Autobiography of
A. R. DOWNER,

Champion Sprinter of the World.

AND

SHORT BIOGRAPHICAL SKETCHES

OF

E. C. BREDIN (WITH HIS IDEAS ON TRAINING),

LEN HURST, FRED BACON, GEORGE BLENNER-HASSET TINCLER,

WITH

METHOD OF TRAINING IN THE EARLY PART OF THE PRESENT CENTURY,

AND

NOTES ON TRAINING FOR BOYS.

The Naval & Military Press Ltd

Published by

The Naval & Military Press Ltd
Unit 5 Riverside, Brambleside
Bellbrook Industrial Estate
Uckfield, East Sussex
TN22 1QQ England

Tel: +44 (0)1825 749494

www.naval-military-press.com
www.nmarchive.com

In reprinting in facsimile from the original, any imperfections are inevitably reproduced and the quality may fall short of modern type and cartographic standards.

BY WAY OF PREFACE.

A famous writer once said that a preface always savoured too much of an apology for his taste. I have no desire to apologise for my literary efforts, but if I have been at all guilty of egotism in the writing of this narrative, I humbly crave the pardon of my readers, and ask them if it can be possible to write of one's self and yet not egotise ?

A. R. D.

INDEX.

PART I.

		PAGE
CHAPTER	I.—SCHOOL DAYS	3
,,	II.—HOW I TOOK TO RUNNING	6
,,	III.—TRAINING TEN YEARS AGO	8
,,	IV.—MY FIRST YEAR IN THE SCOTTISH CHAMPIONSHIPS	10
,,	V.—MY FIRST MEETING WITH CHARLIE BRADLEY	15
,,	VI.—MY FIRST MEETING WITH BRADLEY FROM SCRATCH	18
,,	VII.—I AM MATCHED WITH E. C. BREDIN	23
,,	VIII.—PURITY OF AMATEURISM	25
,,	IX.—AMATEUR AND PROFESSIONAL TRAINING CONTRASTED	30
,,	X.—AMATEUR RACES IN GENERAL	32
,,	XI.—I TURNED PROFESSIONAL	38
,,	XII.—MY FIRST MATCH WITH MILLS	43
,,	XIII.—I RUN CROSS AT EDINBURGH	45
,,	XIV.—FIRST HANDICAP AT POWDERHALL	47
,,	XV.—THE NEWCASTLE SWEEPSTAKES	49
,,	XVI.—I MEET BREDIN AT A QUARTER	53
,,	XVII.—A HOLIDAY AT PROFESSIONAL MEETINGS	60
,,	XVIII.—THE GREATEST RACE I EVER RAN	67
,,	XIX.—MY FIRST DEFEAT IN A MONEY MATCH	70
,,	XX.—AN ENFORCED REST	75
,,	XXI.—MATCHES AGAINST HUTCHINS, KEANE, AND BREDIN	79
,,	XXII.—CHARLES HARPER VANQUISHED	84
,,	XXIII.—ON TRAINING: ADVICE TO YOUNG RUNNERS	89
,,	XXIV.—NOTES ON MY TRAINERS	98

PART II.

CHAPTER	I.—EDGAR CHICHESTER BREDIN	102
,,	II.—TRAINING NOTES BY E. C. BREDIN	108
,,	III.—LEN HURST	112
,,	IV.—TRAINING NOTES BY LEN HURST	117
,,	V.—FRED E. BACON	120
,,	VI.—GEORGE BLENNER-HASSET TINCLER	124
,,	VII.—METHOD OF TRAINING IN THE EARLY PART OF THE PRESENT CENTURY	131
,,	VIII.—METHOD OF TRAINING, ETC. (Continued)	140
,,	IX.—TRAINING NOTES FOR BOYS	144

INDEX TO ILLUSTRATIONS.

	PAGE
J. RICKERBY, ESQ.	FRONTISPIECE.
ALF. R. DOWNER	2
C. A. BRADLEY	13
A. R. DOWNER AT PISTOL PRACTICE	19
H. WATKINS	39
JOE GIBSON. ESQ.	65
HARRY HUTCHINS	77
T. F. KEANE	81
C. HARPER	85
A. R. DOWNER—GET ON YOUR MARK	91
A. R. DOWNER—GET READY	95
A. R. DOWNER—BEATING EVEN TIME	99
E. C. BREDIN	103
LEN HURST	113
F. E. BACON	121
G. B. TINCLER	125
W. G. GEORGE	129
W. SANDERTON, "TREACLE."	133
W. CUMMINGS	137
H. CULLUM	145

A. R. Downer
World's Champion Sprint to Quarter Mile.

· · RUNNING · ·
RECOLLECTIONS

AUTOBIOGRAPHY OF A. R. DOWNER

CHAPTER I.

School Days.

In a certain little Jamaica village the writer of these pages first saw the light of day. My grandfather was a medical man of some importance in the island. Previous, however, to his taking up the study of medicine, he had held a commission as ensign in the 3rd York Regiment. My maternal grandfather was a colonel in the militia, and, among other appointments, held that of Governor of the Penitentiary at Kingston. At the time of my birth, my father held the office of superintendent of police. In the November of 1875, I being then exactly one year and ten months' old, my mother was compelled to take up her residence in this country. In 1880, she finally went to Edinburgh, where, with the exception of a year or so, she has resided ever since.

I was educated at Watson's College, Edinburgh, Portsmouth Grammar School, and the Edinburgh Institution. Watson's, admirable place of education though it may be, filled my childish soul with loathing. The only part of my school life that I cared about was the approach of the annual school games. At only one of these was I allowed to compete, although I was a scholar there for nearly five years. Once I was prostrated by a severe illness, and again, while taking part with some youthful companions in some races beforehand, I strained my heart, and my mother, backed up by the doctor, forbade me to run.

I remember the latter occasion well, though it is as long as 13 years ago. My mother, to make sure, hid my "running things." Nothing daunted, I went down to the ground and tried to borrow some. My efforts proved unsuccessful, and upon my presenting myself for the "100, under 14," in my ordinary clothes, I was indignantly asked where my "uniform" was. Not liking to admit that it had been hidden by my fond parent, I invented some excuse, which, however, was of no avail, and I was requested to remove myself from the track. I did. I went home and wept bitterly.

At Watson's, nevertheless, I pulled off my first race. In the year of grace, 1885, I won the 100 yards for boys under 13. The year after I ran at the Inter-Scholastic Sports, which were open to all Scottish schools, and again proved successful, breaking the tape two yards ahead of another Watson's boy, one Johnny Curry by name.

I was then sent to Portsmouth Grammar School to be coached for a naval appointment, and remained there nearly two years. At this time I was very small for my age, standing barely 4ft. 9in. I ran at the school sports, which took place on the Saturday previous to Jubilee Day, and

I managed to get third in the "150 handicap open." My prize was, of all things, a spirit flask, hardly a suitable sort of prize for a boy of 14!

The next year I was taken away from Portsmouth on account of my house-master leaving the school, and was then sent to the Institution at Edinburgh. Here I ran at the school sports, which I don't think I would have missed for a pension. That I was still of very small stature will be readily understood when I mention that I won the hurdle race for boys under 5ft. That was the only prize I ever won over the sticks, either at school or elsewhere. It must not be imagined that foot running was the only sport that engrossed my attention at school. While at school in Edinburgh I was an ardent and active supporter of the football clubs of both schools, and at Portsmouth I was the smallest boy in the third eleven (football), and I even played for the third eleven at cricket upon one occasion. This was at Ryde, in the Isle of Wight, playing against the Isle of Wight College, when I fielded long-stop.

My school days terminated with my exam. in 1889 for the post of an Engineer student in the Navy, when, I regret to say, I was most ignominiously "ploughed."

CHAPTER II.

How I Took to Running.

SHORTLY after my failure, I went to learn engineering in Glasgow, where I was apprenticed to the firm of G. and A. Harvey, engineers and millwrights. Our manager soon impressed upon me the fact that athletic exercises and engineering had nothing in common. I dare say that is true enough, for I tried to combine the two with disastrous effects—to my engineering career. My friend the manager once told me that if I put as much energy into my work as I did into my running I would do. He also remarked that he wanted to "instil me with a proper spirit."

To begin with, however, I was always a lively kind of youngster—ever ready to take part in any of the impromptu games got up by the men in the meal hours. Football was then, as now, all the rage amongst the working classes of Glasgow. Every meal hour, a few devotees of the sport would be found on a waste piece of ground adjacent to the works, playing a rough-and-tumble game with a ball of a more or less antediluvian appearance. In these said rough-and-tumble games of football my speed was first made apparent to other people. One of the men prophesied that if I "stuck in" and trained, I would one day become a champion. The same man put me in the way of becoming a member of the Rangers' Football Club. The Rangers then had an excellent running track, although, for the benefit of cyclists, it is now banked up out of all recognition.

I do not mean this narrative to be merely an account of every race in which I have competed, although at the end of Part I. of the story will be found a table arranged, as nearly as possible, in "detail order." I shall, therefore, with your permission, proceed to another chapter, in which I purpose to relate the manner in which I, as a youth of 17, used to train.

CHAPTER III.

Training Ten Years Ago.

I related in my last chapter that through the instrumentality of one of the men in the works, I became a member of the Rangers' Football Club. This was merely with the idea of training on the track. Johnny Taylor was then the trainer of the football club, and a cheerier man never breathed. He took an interest in me from the first, and that interest continued till his death some years ago.

Upon my presenting myself at Ibrox Park one fine evening in the spring of 1890, Taylor enquired of me what I wanted. Producing my member's card, of which I was immensely proud (I had paid 15s. for it), I explained that I had come for the purpose of training. His manner changed at once, and he positively beamed.

"Can ye run?" he enquired.

I remarked that I felt justified in believing I could.

"Ah, weel, we'll see. Get yer cla'es off."

I did so, and also impressed the bold John very favourably with my first performance.

Taylor, however, at this time, was too busy with the footballers to pay much attention to the running men, especially to such a novice as myself. I was, therefore, left pretty much to my own devices.

Thus I was in training—such training. My work necessitated my rising at 5.30 every morning, and, with the exception of three-quarters-of-an-hour for breakfast and an hour for dinner, I was kept pretty hard at work all day. In spite of this, I was at Ibrox Park every evening about 7.30, ready to run with all and sundry who requested my services.

Upon one occasion I had had three or four cracks with the pistol, and had run a hundred yards trial with Johnny Gow, who was one of the best local men at the time, when somebody came into the dressing-room and asked for company for half-a-mile. I at once expressed my willingness, and went the distance with him. I may mention that the distance nearly did for me, and I think that this was the only time that I have ever attempted to run half-a-mile either in public or private—as an amateur.

During my first season I managed to win a couple of seconds, and felt that my training (?) had not altogether been in vain. I broke down at the end of the year, but, as the season was practically over, this was of small account. During my whole athletic career I have only been penalised once for getting over my mark before the pistol was fired, and this was in my first season, in the second race I ever ran in—at the Heart of Midlothian Sports, in 1890. At this meeting I won my heat, although I was penalised, and was second in the second round, but was denied my place in the final on account of a wrong number being hoisted.

This reminds me of an amusing incident that happened in a heat in which I was once engaged at the West of Scotland Harriers' Sports. One of the competitors, upon removing his coat at the mark, presented an appearance which might have been expected of a South Sea Islander. He was allowed to run only on condition that he turned out in the second round, if he won his heat, clad in another and more respectable costume, and that he WASHED HIS LEGS. He did not win his heat—so that he was saved the use of soap and water for that day

CHAPTER IV.

My First Year in the Scottish Championships.

Till I reached the age of twenty I lacked that quality which has stood me in good stead upon many an occasion since—I refer to staying power.

I remember once at Falkirk, after the final of a 220, I felt fairly dead beat—so much so, that I really thought I was done for, till I found myself in the dressing-room with a little breath still left in my body. Even now my wind— or rather the want of that desirable commodity—is the chief hindrance to my success at distances over 300 yards. However, I manage to do without it fairly well, and one must be thankful for small mercies as well as for great.

My lack of staying power was much discussed by the athletic press of both Edinburgh and Glasgow, prior to the decision of the Scottish Championships of 1893. Writers in the former city averred that I would not only win the 100 yards, but the 220 and 440 to boot. That was only, probably, because I belonged, in a certain sense, to Edinburgh. The Glasgow Press, on the other hand, maintained that I had not "a dead dog's chance" in any one of the three events. That was because I was not a Glaswegian. A certain athletic paper proceeded to demonstrate that I possessed neither the speed nor the physique to carry me through the training necessary to win a championship, and further stated that "what little running Downer possessed he had learnt at Glasgow when training on Ibrox Park!"

The eventful day was the 17th of June, and Hampden Park, Glasgow, was the venue. I recollect the occasion as

well as though it were yesterday. A friend and myself
made the journey to Glasgow on the Friday afternoon. I
remember this, because we played billiards till four o'clock
on the Saturday morning. Two of the people who were in
that billiard room have since gone the way of all flesh, but
a certain gentleman, now connected with the sporting press
in Manchester, was also there, and I have no doubt will
bear out my statement. I woke later in the morning as
fresh as the proverbial daisy, and ate a hearty breakfast.
My old trainer, Jimmy Duckworth, arrived from Edinburgh
shortly after breakfast, and a move was made for Ibrox
Park—my old training ground—to take the stiffness out of
my legs. Dinner followed—a substantial dinner, I should
say, for I was hungry, and I always believe in satisfying the
cravings of the inner man.

The first event on the programme was the 100 yards.
There were three other competitors—D. R. M'Culloch, who
was then champion of Scotland; M'Lean, who styled himself
"champion of Egypt"; and W. Kerr, of the West of
Scotland Football Club. We got away to a grand start—at
least, so the papers said—but I saw nothing of the other
three till I had broken the worsted.

The 220 yards was a repetition of the sprint, except that
I won by two or three yards more. The Edinburgh papers
declared that I won the sprint by eight, and the 220 by ten
yards. The Glasgow Press, however, made the verdict four
and five yards, respectively.

The 440 yards was nothing more than a worrying match,
and I did my share of the worrying.

I won; poor old M'Culloch was second for the third time
that day.

That was a royal night in Edinburgh! Everybody seemed
to go mad. I was carried shoulder high from the Waverley

Station to a certain hostelry, and there—well, I won't say what happened. The cups were filled to the brim several times, and drained as often, and that ought to suffice. The Glasgow Press was naturally rather wild at having their predictions upset, but I cared very little for that, and still less for the scathing (?) remarks made by the publication to which I have already referred, about what it was pleased to term my gallery running.

The same three championships I retained in 1894 in a similar manner, except that my times in 1894 were rather faster than in 1893, especially the 440, which I won in 51 4-5sec., as against 53 2-5sec. in the previous year. M'Culloch was second again in the 100 and 220, but had to be content with third place in the 440. These championships were run at Powderhall, Edinburgh, on a pouring wet day.

The year 1895 again found me competing for championship honours, and I again won all three events. My cousin, J. K. Ballantyre, ran second to me in the 100 and 220, and R. A. Bruce was behind me in the 440. That 440 was my last Scottish championship, as I stood down in 1896 for my cousin, but he could only win the 100 and 220, so the 440 perforce passed out of the family.

Later on in the same year (1895), I was asked to assist Scotland in their first international athletic contest against Ireland. I did so, and won the 100 yards in 10secs., the 220 in $22\frac{1}{4}$secs., and the 440 in 51 1-5secs. Two of these times, viz., the 100 and 440, tied with Scottish records, and the 220 established a new record for the distance.

I went to New York in the same year with the London Athletic Club team, but our visit has been described often enough, and by abler pens than mine. Suffice it to say, that we went over with four admittedly first-class men—one of whom was a cripple—and we got a thorough good beating.

Gregson, Photo.] [Blackpool.

C. A. BRADLEY.
Established a Record by Winning the Amateur Sprint Championship Four Years consecutively, 1892 to 1895.

CHAPTER V.

My First Meeting with Charlie Bradley.

The St. Bernard's Football Club have long been noted for the excellence of their annual sports, alike for the value of their prizes and the attractions they usually manage to secure. In the season of 1893 they brought down two English champions—Sid Thomas and Charlie Bradley. The former competed in the preliminary meeting held on the Thursday previous to the "big day," and succeeded in breaking a Scottish record. I also lowered the figures for the 220 to 22 4-5sec. on the same day—a feat which stirred the somewhat apathetic Edinburgh crowd to something like enthusiasm. My appearance on the following Saturday was eagerly waited for. Bradley was down to give me three yards start in 120, and as we had never met before, considerable interest was attached to our struggle. I was advised by some well-meaning, though somewhat officious, friends to eschew my allowance and start off the same mark as the English champion. I replied, that had the handicapper seen fit to place me on the same mark as Bradley, I would have only been too pleased to test my speed against his. As it was, I would try my best to beat him every time we met till at last I could do so level.

In this, my first race with Bradley, we both won our heats, and to the accompaniment of a great shout from the crowd the final was decided. Bradley caught me with about 20 yards to go, and just beat Lander (10) for first place, while I was inches to the rear of the latter. It was a peculiar thing that my first race with Bradley should have been run at Edinburgh and my last at Huddersfield, two places with which we were each identified.

My next meet with Bradley took place at Powderhall, in the following year, in a "match." The Huddersfield man was to give me three yards start in 100. He was successful in this, but I turned the tables on him in the 120, wherein I was in receipt of three-and-a-half yards. As in the previous year, we both got through our heats, but the result was widely different, as I was given the decision by half-a-yard.

Bradley and I met again later on that year at Celtic Park, Glasgow, in a 120 Invitation Handicap. That was the funniest race I ever took part in, both as regards handicapping and the issue. The handicap was framed by a gentleman who would never give in that I was as fast as I was made out to be, but, as I have said before, I was not a "Glaswegian." Accordingly he placed me on the four yards' mark, although I had previously beaten Bradley with three-and-a-half. Whether it was prejudice or ignorance that was responsible for the action I know not, but there the fact remains. In the race, Max Wittenberg had two-and-a-quarter, Teddy Messenger six-and-a-half, and Gallagher, of Ireland, seven. I believe that Joe Magee, the Irish three-quarter back, was on seven yards also. Poor old Bob Hindle was pistol firer. Bob had a style of starting all his own. He believed in talking soothingly to the men. "Noo, lads," he used to say, "get a' nicely set, noo, staand steady, nicely set, nicely "——Bang ! Upon this occasion he was in the middle of this speech when someone in white went flying past me. "Bang" went the gun, and I went after the object in white. The crowd were furious, and hooted and shouted like fiends, until at last Bradley consented to run the race again. This action on his part was much applauded by the spectators, who a few minutes before had expressed their disapprobation in a manner more forcible than polite.

Upon the run-off the same speech was made by Bob Hindle, and we were "a' nicely set" awaiting the report. This never came, and at last "Teddy" Messenger could stand it no longer. He slowly raised himself, turned round, and favoured poor old Bob with a bit of the choicest Lancashire dialect. The rest of us waited till he had finished, and Bob once again told us to get "a' nicely set." He made no mistake this time, and we got away to an excellent start. I won. Messenger was second, and Bradley and Wittenberg dead heated for third place. I asked Bob afterwards why he had kept us waiting so long. Quoth he, "Weel, ye see, I was wantin' tae mak' sairtin that nane o' you lads was gaun for a flyer like that felly Bradley did."

That was the last time I ever met Bradley on handicap terms. The next occasion we ran against each other was at Stamford Bridge, in the Essex Beagles' 100 Yards Scratch. That incident, however, deserves a new chapter.

I should mention that I had long since given up any idea of shining in the engineering line, and had been "ploughed" several times for various Civil Service appointments.

CHAPTER VI.

My First Meeting with Bradley from Scratch.

In the spring of 1895 I left Edinburgh to seek my fortune. After some little trouble, I succeeded in getting a situation as a traveller for disinfectants. My ground was to be the South Coast of England, and the principal places I was to call at were hotels, restaurants, etc. Brighton was the first town in which I tried to push my wares, but after exhausting the list of hotels with which I had been furnished with no success, I came to the natural conclusion that it was time for me to seek some vocation other than that of "disinfectant monger." I therefore flung my samples over the Brighton pier in disgust, and went back to my hotel to ruminate. After pondering over my circumstances, I concluded that the best thing I could do was to stay in Brighton and train for the Essex Beagles' Sports, which were shortly coming off. Hence every day I was practising busily at Preston Park in company with Godfrey Shaw, who was then resident at Hayward's Heath. I left Brighton on the morning of the sports—to be accurate, on May 4, 1895—and Shaw and I proceeded to Stamford Bridge.

In the first heat, Bradley and Wittenberg ran first and second respectively, and in the other Thomas and myself finished in like order. I remember I nearly lost my place in the final by being a little too clever. Having gone 50 yards, and finding myself well in front, I waited for Thomas, and all but let Calder, who was on my other side, beat me for second place. I never tried THAT trick again. In the final I made no mistake; I went from the crack of

A. R. DOWNER AT PISTOL PRACTICE.
BILL BOTT (TRAINER).

the pistol to the bitter end, and eventually won by about two yards from Bradley, Thomas just beating Wittenberg for third place by a foot, a yard and a half to Bradley's rear. I will now give a list of races in which Bradley and myself have met.

BRADLEY v. DOWNER.

Name of Sports.	Year.	Dis. in Yards.	Downer's start.	Result.	Time.
Edin. St. Bernard's	1893	120 cndrs	3	Bradley	$11\frac{4}{5}$
Edin. St Bernard's	1894	120 cndrs	$3\frac{1}{2}$	Downer	$12\frac{1}{5}$
Edin. St. Bernard's	1894	100 cndrs	3	Bradley	$10\frac{1}{5}$
Celtic F.C., Glasgow	1894	120 grass	4	Downer	$11\frac{4}{5}$
Essex Beagl s	1895	100 cndrs	scr	Downer	10
Halifax	1895	135 grass	scr	Bradley	—
Lancaster	1895	100 grass	scr	Bradley	$10\frac{1}{5}$
Crewe	1895	100 cndrs	scr	Bradley	$10\frac{1}{5}$
A.A.A. Champ. (Lndn)	1895	100 cndrs	scr	Bradley	10
Edin St Bernard's	1895	120 cndrs	scr	Downer	$12\frac{1}{5}$
Royton	1895	100 grass	scr	Bradley	$10\frac{1}{5}$
Royton	1895	110 grass	scr	Downer	—
Stoke-upon-Trent	1895	100 cndrs	scr	dead heat	10
Ditto (run off)	1895	100 cndrs	scr	dead heat	$9\frac{4}{5}$
Clitheroe F.C.	1896	100 grass	scr	Downer	—
Clitheroe F.C.	1896	100 grass	scr	Downer	—
South London Har.	1896	100 grass	scr	Bradley	—
South London Har.	1896	75 grass	scr	Bradley	$7\frac{4}{5}$
Notts Forest	1896	100 grass	scr	Bradley	$10\frac{1}{5}$
Edin. Pharmacy A.C.	1896	120 cndrs	scr	Downer	12
Manningham F.C.	1896	100 grass	scr	Bradley	$10\frac{1}{5}$
Lancaster	1896	100 grass	scr	Bradley	$10\frac{1}{5}$
Barrow-in-Furness	1896	100 cndrs	scr	Downer	10
Halifax	1896	120 grass	scr	Bradley	—
Crewe Alexandra	1896	100 cndrs	scr	Bradley	10
Huddersfield	1896	100 grass	scr	Bradley	$10\frac{1}{5}$

Very few of these races require any description. As a general rule, Bradley would be from one yard to six inches in front at 50 yards, and I would then begin to pull in the slack, usually beating him just after the 100 yards mark.

I do not wish to make excuses for my defeat in the 100 Yards Championship in 1895, the only event of the sort in which I ever took part, but I think I could have given Bradley a much better race for it had it not been for an unfortunate occurrence a fortnight prior to the eventful day. I happened to be running at Powderhall grounds in the St. George's Football Club Sports. I had won my heat in the 300, and a friend begged me to do my best in the final, as, to use his own elegant expression, "He had got his last shilling on, and would be broke till the next blue moon." Whether it was the thought of his losses or not I do not know, but I got home. I had to pay for it, though, and in this wise. I had previously gone through three heats of the sprint, and, as can easily be imagined, I was feeling pretty well fagged. Five yards from home I was only fourth, a yard behind the leader. I made one great effort, however, and broke the worsted a few inches in front of the second man. I nearly broke my neck as well, for I fell heavily to the ground, peeling the skin off my left elbow and knee in the most shocking manner. I could not run for nearly a week afterwards, and fancy that this mishap greatly interfered with any chance I might have had of winning the championship.

CHAPTER VII.

I am Matched with E. C. Bredin.

NEXT to Bradley, Bredin figures as having run the greatest number of races with me. Our first meeting was at the West of Scotland Harriers' Sports in 1894. He and I were matched to run 250 yards on level terms for a gold watch. Bredin was greatly fancied for this event by the promoting body; but even in those days I was a good match-maker, and won by seven or eight yards in 26 1-5sec. We did not again meet till the spring of the following year, at Kennington Oval, in the South London Harriers' Sports, upon which occasion we ran 350 yards. Neither of us should have competed, as Bredin was only half-trained, and I had been getting into condition to run Bradley 120 yards at the same meeting. The last-named, however, did not turn up, and the committee appealed to us in desperation. I wanted to run 300 yards, but "with great magnanimity"—this is a critic's expression, not mine—gave in, and we ran 350. I made the mistake, which I have never done since, of allowing Bredin to make the running, trusting to my superior finish to beat him in the run in. The latter, however, has such long legs, that I had to keep too far behind him, and was thus giving away too much when we entered the straight. In the end I was beaten by half-a-yard.

Our next meeting was at Glasgow, about two months' later, in a 300 yards match at sports promoted by the West of Scotland Harriers. This time I led all the way, and won by nine or ten yards in 31 2-5sec., which established a new amateur world's record.

A 350 yards scratch race at Crewe on the following Saturday was our fourth and last meeting as amateurs.

Upon this occasion there were two other competitors—Jones, of Shrewsbury, and Taylor. Profiting by my lesson earlier in the year, I made all the running, and won by two yards from Bredin, with Taylor third.

Other athletes with whom I had "matches" in my amateur days were Teddy Messenger and S. R. Huson, of London. I met Messenger over 200 yards at Powderhall in the St. Bernard's Sports, 1894, and beat him by a yard-and-a-half. Huson and I came together over 200 yards at the South London Harriers' Sports in September, 1894. I was originally matched to run Bredin 350 yards, but owing to that unfortunate pedestrian spraining his ankle about a week before the date fixed for the sports, the South London Harriers prevailed upon Huson to take his place and run me 200. This he did, but I won somewhat more easily than they expected, owing, I presume, to his not being as fit as he might have been.

Wittenberg and I never were great rivals, although we frequently met in level races. Our first meeting was in 1893, at Blackburn, in a 220 yards' handicap. We were both off the four yards' mark, but while I ran second he was unplaced. We tested our paces for the second time in Glasgow in the following spring. Here he beat me in a 120 yards' handicap, giving me one yard start. Our next encounter was at Glasgow, later on in the same year, when he had to give me one-and-three-quarter yards' start. I have already described the race in the preceding chapter. During the following two years we repeatedly met in scratch sprint races, and he was always a good third to Bradley or myself. Our last meeting was at Huddersfield, in the 220 Yards N.C.A.A. Championship, which, by the way, was my last race as an amateur. Here I won, with Wittenberg second, and Bradley third.

CHAPTER VIII.

PURITY OF AMATEURISM.

IN 1895 my presence at athletic gatherings invariably proved a big draw, generally for the reason that I was the only man who could give Bradley a race in a level 100 yards, but often because I could run any distance from 100 yards to 440. Hence I was the recipient of many inducements to appear at the various meetings throughout the country. These transactions were generally negotiated through a third person. For instance, my presence might be desired at, let us say, "Muddletown." The "Muddletown" secretary would go to a friend of mine and perhaps remark :—

"I believe you know Downer, don't you?"

"Slightly," would probably be remarked.

"Do you think you could get him to run at our sports?"

If my friend were at all acquainted with the secretary, he would take him aside, and say : "Look here ; what will you give him?"

A sum having been stated, my friend would communicate with me, and the affair would be settled to the satisfaction of all parties. Often, however, the secretary, or some other member of his committee, would be deputed to wait upon me with a view to securing me for their sports. He would, perhaps, be allowed to run to a certain sum, and if that did not satisfy my requirements, the deal would be off. This was a very simple way of doing business, and committees of sports-holding clubs would do well to take notice. I do not mind putting them up to a wrinkle or two now that I am out of the running. "Carte blanche" on the deputy's part was what I liked. A certain gentleman (this was in my professional days, however,) was once requested to try and get me over for some sports in a certain town, and to spare no expense. I had previously, however, signed an agreement with another club binding myself not to compete in that town prior to the latter club's sports. Thus I was compelled to decline, and to sacrifice a retaining fee that would have kept a small but happy family for a month of Sundays.

I was running at some sports at Manningham once, just after I had scored my first victory over Bradley, and the secretary of a Yorkshire cricket or football club approached me, and held out various inducements for me to turn out at their sports. I was not very keen about it, as doing so would have necessitated my throwing up a situation which I then held in the Metropolis. After a great deal of talk, we arranged that I was to wire my decision in two days, stating what fee I should require.

On the following Monday, therefore, I wired up, "10, Downer."

The telegram came back, "6, F—."

I then wired, "8 at least, Downer."

The reply came—" All right, 8."

I went and competed, but won nothing, Bradley beating me for third place in a handicap.

The following year, '96, I had an interview with Mr. "F—," and he beat me down to £5 5s. However, I got a second prize, valued at £4, so I did fairly well.

By the way, there was an awful row about my running at Halifax that year. The 100 Yards N.C.A.A. Championship was decided at Southport the same day, and a lot of clever people could only find one reason for my running at the former place. "Oh, the Southport people would give him nothing," they would say, "and he's getting paid to run at

Halifax." As a matter of fact, I ran at Halifax, in preference to Southport, because I was ineligible to compete in the 100 Yards N.C.A.A. Championship, while at the former meeting I stood a good chance to win the 220 Yards Invitation Handicap.

I could have got good value at Southport, as the N.C.A.A. medals are supposed to be worth £5, and one can always realise £4 on them !

The meanest trick I was ever served in my amateur-professional days was by a certain Lancashire Harriers' Club in 1896. They had a week-day meeting, and sent a representative to get me to run if possible. I was not over keen about turning out, and put my usual blunt question to the ambassador—" What will you give me?" He said that if I left it to his committee I would not be disappointed. I agreed to this, and after the sports asked the diplomatist when his committee intended to settle with me. He named a place, and promised to be there at ten o'clock that evening. He kept his appointment, but informed me that his committee had not reckoned up the gate-money and balanced the expenses. I might expect to hear from him shortly, when he would enclose my share of the "gate." He never wrote, but I met him a few days afterwards, and he informed me that his committee had decided not to give me anything. In other words, they would sooner break their word than a law of the all-powerful A.A.A. ! Could anyone imagine anything meaner? I had put myself to serious inconvenience to run at a very third-rate meeting, naturally expecting to be paid for it, instead of which I was considerably out of pocket, after helping to fill the coffers of a club with which I had nothing whatever to do.

There were certain sports at which I was only too glad to run for nothing—such as the London Athletic Club the

Civil Service, and Huddersfield—but very few others; in fact, there were few sports at which I ran, and at which I was not paid. And yet the clubs promoting these sports are some of them recognised as affiliated to the A.A.A., while others are allowed to hold sports under their rules and auspices.

The Burnley Cricket Club, whose evidence very materially helped to "string up" five of the finest "amateur" runners in England, had arranged to pay me £8. One of the officials asked me if I would not reduce the sum, and take £6, as Bradley had done so. This I declined to do, as I had had a very hard afternoon's work, and, moreover, they had had a good gate. I think I was quite justified in this action, more especially as I had had numerous offers made to me by other clubs for the same date.

One of the first questions I was asked, when being examined by the A.A.A., was: "Did you receive a sum of money for running at Burnley?"

There is no doubt that a lot of clubs at that time turned "Queen's evidence" to save their own skins. People may put me down as being spiteful, and no doubt they would be right, but I was brought face to face with so much meanness at that time, that I became thoroughly disgusted with both amateurs and their legislators. I did not mind being suspended, as the A.A.A. are not the rulers of the universe, or even of athletics; but I was not unnaturally indignant at the fact of being debarred from competing with gentlemen (?) amateurs, while the very clubs who had paid me to come and run at their sports should be allowed to go scot-free. I place the query after the word "gentlemen" purposely, for how many amateurs—that is, amateurs according to the definition of the Association's term—are, or even profess to be, gentlemen? As a matter of fact, 99 per cent. of them are not even amateurs according to the literal translation of the word. I do not wish to be accused of making statements at random, so I will endeavour to make my meaning clear. How many so-called amateurs run for the pure love of the sport? Do not the most, in fact, by far the most, enter and try to win only at those meetings where the best prizes are given, and, in many cases, where there is the most gambling? I do not blame them—far from it—but I do condemn the smug hypocrisy of the governing body who recognise these things, and, knowing them to be contrary to their laws, make no attempt to prevent them, because they know that by doing so they will only bring about their own undoing.

When the Athletic Association limit the prizes given at meetings run under their auspices to parchment certificates, or, at most, bronze medals, they will be justly entitled to the name of "amateur." People may say that no runner would bother about running for the honour of winning a piece of paper or twopennyworth of copper, and that, if these things came to pass, the result would be a strike in the ranks of amateurs.

CHAPTER IX.

Amateur and Professional Training Contrasted.

I have often been asked to describe how it was that I came to show such a vast improvement in my form after I turned professional. The reason is very simple. When I train for a race now, I am not galloping all over the country, running all sorts of distances. Instead, I remain quietly in my quarters, never throwing a chance away. I do not mean to say that I never run in any handicaps during a preparation, but I take good care that when I do I come to no harm thereby. A glance at the following table, during the time I resided in London, will give you an idea of the amount of travelling I did, and the races I used to run in my amateur-professional days:—

Date.	Place.	Races run.	Distance from former place.
May 24	Situated in London...	—	—
May 25	Manningham	100 yards	200 miles
May 25	Armley	100 yards	
May 28	Edinburgh	150 yards	200 miles
May 28	,,	120 yards (3)	
June 1	Halifax	135 yards	200 miles
June 1	,,	120 yards	
June 3	London	120 yards (2)	200 miles
June 3	,,	300 yards	
June 4	Lancaster	120 yards (2)	240 miles
June 4	,,	100 yards	
June 8	London	120 yards (2)	240 miles
June 10	Glasgow	100 yards (2)	400 miles
June 10	,,	300 yards	
June 11	Edinburgh	—	50 miles
June 12	Cambridge	100 yards	330 miles
June 12	London	—	70 miles
June 15	Crewe	100 yards	130 miles
June 15	,,	120 yards (2)	—
June 15	,,	350 yards	—
June 22	Edinburgh	—	270 miles
		Total	2,530 miles

(2) Signifies two heats.   (3) Signifies three heats.

It will thus be seen, that in one month, I had travelled upwards of 2,500 miles, and before that year was out, I had completed 5,000 miles in this country alone. Changes of water, air, beds, and food, are bound to affect any man, still more so one who is expected to be in the "pink of condition" at every meeting at which he runs. Besides, at that time, I could rightly have been described as being "of no fixed residence." I was sometimes for a week at a time without putting my pumps on. How I ran, as well as I did, is a marvel to me. I suppose I used to have a happy knack of throwing all trouble on one side in those days, and probably that fact helped to counteract the effects of my mode of life. I can always run best when my mind is easy, and I think everybody can do their best in a like condition. This applies more to pedestrians, than to people in any other calling, because, especially in sprint running, one wants to feel as lively as possible. I remember once I was running a trial at Powderhall shortly before the New Year Handicap of 1897. As I walked on to the ground, I was handed a letter bearing a most unpleasant intimation. I ran my trial, but did so badly that my backers decided not to back me for the Handicap, but backed my trial horse instead. He got beaten in his heat, and I won mine in two yards faster time than I had run in my trial. Then there was a fine to-do! I was accused of not doing my best in my trial, of wanting to throw my backers over, of having some other men backing me to whom I was giving information, and of——I don't know how many crimes. All this, because I happened to feel off colour in my trial. I told my backers that the best thing they could do now was to back me for the final, which they did. But, alas, for human hopes, I was beaten in the second round!

CHAPTER X.

AMATEUR RACES IN GENERAL.

BEFORE concluding this, the first part of my story, I should like to make a few general remarks upon amateur races. I do not mean to say that amateur sports in this country are lacking in good management, but still there is room for vast improvement. There are two officials at the average athletic meeting who generally fall short of proficiency in their duties. I refer to the starter and referee. I mentioned a case earlier in this production, where the starter twice bungled over one single race, and this is by no means a unique experience in my career. I have been at sports where the starter walked on to the ground with a regular armoury slung round his person, but never an honest muzzle-loading pistol among the lot. He had two or three revolvers and a saloon pistol, for which, he remarked to me in confidence, he had only ball cartridges, but that he wouldn't use it unless he ran short of his other ammunition. I admit a good "barker" is very hard to get nowadays, but still one would imagine that an official starter would surely be able to possess himself of one.

The referee is often possessed of oblique vision, and, as often as not, it takes about four men to allot a few miserable prizes. I once ran at some sports where they had four judges for the final of the sprint—one for each man. There was a battle-royal after the race. The judge who was to "take" the winner "took" the man whom judge number two gave as being second, and judge number three, who was to fasten on to the third man, was prepared to take his affidavit that the man whom judge number one gave as the winner was only third. That scene was worth going a mile to see. At another meeting I was given as having run a dead-heat with three others. I had been left on my mark owing to the inefficiency of the starter, and I have a very good idea that I was nowhere in the race when the worsted was broken. I was never one, however, to dispute the referee's decision, and won the decider very comfortably. I may mention that this incident happened at about the only sort of place at which one would expect it to occur—at school games. The judges at these functions are usually (as in this case they were) two of the masters at the school, who never see any other sports except those of their own school, and, in consequence, are apt to make the most glaring mistakes.

I recollect once competing at a meeting in, if not exactly the North of Scotland, very near it. The starter had a muzzle-loader right enough, but had not provided himself with powder, trusting to a far-seeing Providence, or the committee, to find him some. We were started by the report of THE CAP ALONE—surely a unique experience at amateur sports. The committee evidently did not know for what purpose worsted was intended, as the winner of each race had to breast a clothes-line before being granted the verdict.

These are only one or two of many such like instances which I have noted in all parts of the country. I now append a list of some of my performances as an amateur.

PRIZES WON IN MY AMATEUR DAYS.

(The figures in brackets refer to my start.)

1885—Watson's College Sports, 100 Yards, open to boys under 13	1st
1886—Edinburgh Inter-Scholastic Sports, 100 Yards, open to boys under 13	1st
1887—Portsmouth Grammar School Sports, 150 Yards Handicap	3rd
1888—Edinburgh Institute Sports. Hurdle Race, under 5ft.	1st
1890—Edinburgh Institute Sports, 300 Yards Handicap (7yds.), open to former pupils	2nd
1890—Glasgow Rangers and Clydesdale Harriers, Open 100 Yards Handicap (10)	1st
1891—Abercorn F.C., Paisley, 100 Handicap. open (6½)	4th
1891—West of Scotland Harriers, 100 Handicap, open (7)	2nd
1891—Edinburgh Institute, 100 Scratch, former pupils	1st
1891—Edinburgh Institute, 100 Scratch. former pupils	1st
1892—Watson's College. 100 Scratch, former pupils	1st
1892—Stewart's College, 100 Handicap, open (scr.)	2nd
1892—Heart of Midlothian F.C., 100 Handicap, open (1½)	1st
1892—Edinburgh Institute, 100 Yards Scratch, former pupils	1st
1892—Edinburgh Institute, 440 Yards Handicap, former pupils. in football costume	2nd
1892—St. Bernard's F.C., Edinburgh, 120 Yards Handicap, open (1½)	2nd
1892—Police Sports, Salford Racecourse, 100 Yards Handicap, open (3½)	3rd
1892—Preston N.E. F.C., 100 Yards Handicap, open (3½)	2nd
1892—Blackley C.C., 100 Handicap, open. Derby Plate (3½)	3rd
1892—East Stirlingshire C.C., Falkirk, 100 Handicap, open (1½)	1st
1893—Edinburgh Harriers, Confined Sports, 300 Handicap (scr.)	1st
1893—West of Scotland C.C., 100 Yards Handicap, open (1)	1st
1893—Watson's College, 100 Handicap, former pupils (scr.)	2nd
1893—Stewart's College, 100 Handicap, open (scr.)	1st
1893—Glasgow Merchants. 100 Yards Handicap, open (1)	2nd
1893—Glasgow Merchants, 220 Yards Handicap, open (3)	2nd
1893—Edinburgh Pharmacy A.C., 120 Yards Handicap, open (scratch), 12½sec., Scottish record	1st
1893—Vale of Leven F.C., 100 Yards Handicap, open (1)	1st
1893—Vale of Leven F.C., 220 Yards Handicap, open (6)	1st
1893—Edinburgh Harriers, 100 Yards Scratch, Muir Cup	1st

1893—Edinburgh Harriers, 120 Yards Handicap, open, 12⅖sec., Scottish record 1st
1893—Scotch Championship Meeting. 100 Yards. 10⅖sec............. 1st
1893—Scotch Championship Meeting, 220 Yards. 23⅖sec............. 1st
1893—Scotch Championship Meeting, 440 Yards, 53⅖sec............. 1st
1893—Edinburgh Institute, 100 Handicap, former pupils (scr.) 1st
1893—Edinburgh University, 120 Yards Handicap, open (scr.)... 1st
1893—St. Bernard's F.C., 220 Yards Handicap, open (scr.)......... 1st
1893—Blackburn Rovers, 220 Yards Handicap, open (4) 2nd
1894—Stewart's College, 100 Yards Handicap, open (scr.) 1st
1894—Heart of Midlothian, 100 Yards Handicap, open (scr.) ... 1st
1894—Glasgow Merchants C.C., 100 Handicap, open (1)............. 3rd
1894—Glasgow Merchants C.C., 220 Handicap, open (scr.)......... 3rd
1894—Edinburgh Pharmacy A.C., 120 Handicap, open (scr.) ... 3rd
1894—W.S.H., 250 Yards Match v. E. C. Bredin, 26⅖sec. 1st
1894—Falkirk F.C., 100 Yards Handicap, open (scr.) 1st
1894—Scotch Championships, 100 Yards, 10⅖sec. 1st
1894—Scotch Championships, 220 Yards, 22⅖sec...................... 1st
1894—Scotch Championships, 440 Yards, 51⅖sec. 1st
1894—Edinburgh Institute, 100 Handicap, former pupils (scr.) 1st
1894—Edinburgh Institute. 300 Handicap, former pupils (scr.) 1st
1894—St. Bernard's F.C., 100 Yards Handicap Match v. Bradley (3) 2nd
1894—St. Bernard's F.C., 120 Yards Handicap. open (3½) 1st
1894—Edinburgh U.H., 120 Yards Handicap, open (scr.) 1st
1894—St. Bernard's F.C., 220 Yards Match v. Messenger 1st
1894—Celtic F.C., 120 Invitation Handicap, Bradley scr. (4) 1st
1894—Celtic F.C., 120 Yards Handicap, open. Bradley scr. (3) ... 3rd
1894—Free Gardeners, Hawkhill, 120 Handicap, open (scr.) 1st
1894—Maypole C.C., 100 Yards Handicap, open (scr.) 3rd
1894—Edin. U.H., Even. Sports, 150 Handicap, open (scr.) 3rd
1894—Arbroath Harriers, 100 Yards Handicap, open (scr.) 1st
1894—South London Harriers, 200 Yards Match v. Huson 1st
1894—South London Harriers, 75 Yards Handicap, open (scr.).. 3rd
1895—Clitheroe, 120 Yards Handicap, open (scr.) 1st
1895—South London Harriers, 100 Yards Handicap (1½)............. 1st
1895—Essex Beagles, 100 Yards Scratch Race, Bradley second, time 10sec... 1st
1895—London A.C., 120 Yards Handicap, open (scr.) 2nd

1895—London A.C., 200 Yards Invitation Handicap (scr.), time $19\frac{7}{10}$sec., record 1st
1895—Finchley Harriers, 120 Yards Handicap, open (scr.) 2nd
1895—Manningham F.C., 100 Scratch Challenge Cup } Same 1st
1895—Armley F.C., 100 Yards Scratch Challenge Cup } day. 1st
1895—Edinburgh Pharmacy A.C., 150 Yards Invitation Handicap (scr.), 15sec., Scotch record 1st
1895—Edinburgh Pharmacy A.C., 120 Yards Handicap, open (scr.) 2nd
1895—Opening Wood Green Track, 120 Handicap, open (scr.) ... 2nd
1895—Lancaster A.C., 100 Yards Scratch, Bradley won 2nd
1895—Lancaster A.C., 100 Yards Handicap (scr.) 2nd
1895—Civil Service Sports, 120 Yards Handicap, open (scr.)...... 2nd
1895—West of Scotland Harriers, 300 Yards Match v. Bredin, time $31\frac{3}{5}$sec., world's amateur record 1st
1895—London A.C. v. Cambridge U.A.C., 100 Yards, for L.A.C. .. 1st
1895—Crewe Alexandra, 100 Yards Scratch (Bradley won) 2nd
1895—Crewe Alexandra, 350 Yards Scratch (Bredin 2nd) 1st
1895—Scottish Championships, 100 Yards, 10sec. 1st
1895—Scottish Championships, 220 Yards, $23\frac{2}{5}$sec. 1st
1895—Scottish Championships, 440 Yards, $52\frac{3}{5}$sec., easily 1st
1895—St. George's F.C., Edinburgh, 120 Handicap, open (scr.)... 3rd
1895—St. George's F.C., Edinburgh, 300 Handicap, open (scr.)... 1st
1895—Wigan Wednesday C.C., 120 Handicap, open (scr.) 1st
1895—A.A.A. Championships, Stamford Bridge, 100 Yards (Bradley won).. 2nd
1895—St. Bernard's F.C., 120 Yards Invitation Handicap (Bradley scr.) (scr.).. 1st
1895—St. Bernard's F.C., 120 Yards Handicap, open (scr.)......... 2nd
1895—Edinburgh University A.C., 220 Yards Handicap, open (scr.), $22\frac{3}{5}$sec. 1st
1895—Scottish A.A.A. v Irish A.A.A., 100 Yards, for S.A.A.A., 10sec. 1st
1895—Scottish A.A.A. v. Irish A.A.A., 220 Yards, for S.A.A.A., $22\frac{1}{4}$sec., Scottish record 1st
1895—Scottish A.A.A. v. Irish A.A.A., 440 Yards, for S.A.A.A., $52\frac{1}{5}$sec. 1st
1895—Edinburgh Harriers, Evening Meeting, 120 Handicap, open (scr.) 3rd
1895—Edinburgh Drapers' Association, 220 Handicap, open (scr.) 1st
1895—Royton, 100 Yards Scratch (Bradley won) 2nd

1895—Royton, 250 Yards Handicap, open (scr.)	1st
1895—Stoke-upon-Trent, 100 Yards Scratch (two dead heats with Bradley)	1st
1895—Burnley, 120 Yards Handicap, open (scr.)	3rd
1895—Burnley, 220 Yards Handicap, open (scr.)	1st
1895—Cliftonville, Belfast, 300 Yards Handicap, open (scr.)	1st
1895—Wigan R.A.O.B., 120 Yards Handicap, open (scr.)	3rd
1896—Clitheroe F.C., 100 Yards Scratch (Bradley 2nd)	1st
1896—Clitheroe F.C., 120 Yards Handicap, open (scr)	1st
1896—South London Harriers, 75 Yards Scratch (Bradley won)	2nd
1896—Notts Forest F.C., 100 Yards Scratch (Bradley won)	2nd
1896—Edinburgh Drapers' Association, 120 Yards Invitation Handicap (Bradley, scr., 2nd)	1st
1896—Edinburgh Drapers' Association, 120 Yards Handicap, open (scr.)	1st
1896—Manningham F.C., 100 Yards Scratch (Bradley 1st)	1st
1896—Lancaster (1st day), 200 Yards Handicap, open (scr.)	3rd
1896—Lancaster (2nd day), 100 Yards Scratch (Bradley won)	2nd
1896—Lancaster (2nd day), 200 Yards Handicap, open (scr.)	3rd
1896—Barrow-in-Furness, 100 Yards Scratch (Bradley 2nd)	1st
1896—Halifax, 220 Yards Invitation Handicap (scr.)	2nd
1896—Crewe Alexandra, 100 Yards Scratch (Bradley won)	2nd
1896—Crewe Alexandra, 220 Yards Handicap, open (scr.)	2nd
1896—Nelson C.C., 120 Yards Handicap, open (scr.)	2nd
1896—Huddersfield, 100 Yards Scratch (Bradley won)	2nd
1896—Huddersfield, 220 Yards, N.C.A.A.A. Championship (Wittenberg 2nd)	1st

CHAPTER XI.

LIKE a bombshell into the midst of the athletic world came the news that Bradley, Bacon, Watkins, Crossland, Blair, and Downer were suspended for ever and a day from competing at amateur sports. To those who were in the know, the news came in a much less abrupt fashion. I myself had been warned for weeks before it really happened. Blair was not very long in getting reinstated, but his brother is a barrister, and pleaded his cause so well, that the dread body saw fit to rescind their action. The association did not offer to pay my expenses up to town, although I had travelled expressly from Lancashire. However, I consider I had fully my money's worth of fun out of the meeting. It was vastly amusing, being sat upon by, and having to answer for my crimes to, my partners in what some idiotic papers termed my "nefarious transactions." I could do very little but laugh the whole time. There was such a sanctimonious look on every face in the room, that one would have thought we were being tried for manslaughter at least. However, this action of the Amateur Athletic Association made a considerable alteration in my life.

I TURNED PROFESSIONAL.

I believe I was the first of the suspendees to take the bull by the horns in this fashion. I was suspended on a Friday night, June 25th, 1896, and on the Monday following I had signed an agreement to run at Gamage's Sports against Charley Barden, the cyclist, on August Bank Holiday. Shortly after my suspension, I thought a short holiday would do me no harm, and I went to Rhyl for a week or two.

Gregson, Photo.] [Blackpool.

H. WATKINS.

One Hour's Record Holder and 4 to 12 miles Champion of the World. Distance covered in one hour, 11 miles 1,286 yards. Turned Professional, 1896.

After my sojourn at Rhyl, I went into semi-training for my match with Barden, which was to be decided over 220 yards, Barden to stand and mount by report of pistol. I beat him, with a yard or two to spare. The remainder of the summer I passed in going round the country, running at Scotch games. These games are highly diverting ; and the crudeness of the arrangements would make the tamest official of the Amateur Athletic Association open his eyes in holy horror. Imagine a rough stubble field, and a " track " staked off thereon about 200 yards to the lap, with square corners, and the going like a switchback railway, and you will get a slight idea of what Scotch games are like. The vileness of the track, however, is only one of the evils. The starts are often paced out, and the member of the band who performs on the drum often officiates in the capacity of starter, his instrument taking the part of a pistol. I have run at games where the signal was given by an individual who waved his handkerchief (a red one) three times, the third time being the signal to " go." On one occasion, in a 120 yards' handicap, we had to turn sharp round a post after 50 yards, the two straights being at an angle of 45 degrees. However, Scotch games are, on the whole, good fun. The best known " peds," as a rule, " stand in " with one another, which means they agree to divide among themselves any prize-money the school may win. The poor " locals," as a rule, have to be content with what is left. This " standing in " robs the games of anything like real sport, there usually being but one trier in each event. In fact, the only tussles are between the regular professional and the poor local, who believes he can run, and insists upon turning out year after year at his own games.

But the starting is the funniest part of the whole affair. No one, who is " on the job," ever dreams of waiting for the report of the pistol, or whatever the signal may be, but is generally running some five yards (this is no exaggeration) when the signal is given.

It is quite a common occurrence, I am sorry to say, for a man to shift his peg up some 20 or 30 yards, even in a quarter-mile race, and stand there looking as meek as possible when the marksman comes to see if he is on his proper mark. I once saw a man, after he had been placed on his mark, go to the railings, apparently to speak to a friend, creep under and come on to the track some yards further up. I went on tour round a few of these meetings with Billy Cross, and Cross, by the way, was one of the most versatile pedestrians that ever ran. From 100 yards to 20 miles this talented gentleman was never disgraced in any company. He was also no small beer over timber, and many a hurdle race he placed to his credit at some of the meetings I have described.

CHAPTER XII.

My First Match with Mills.

In September, 1896, a challenge appeared in the *Sporting Chronicle* from W. S. Mills, of Rochdale, offering me two yards in 150, or three in 200. I looked about me and found a backer in Mr. Robert Beattie, of Edinburgh. I then asked Mills for three yards in 150, or four in 200, for £50 a side. To this he consented, and one day, at the latter end of September, found me *en route* for Manchester with a "tenner" in my pocket from Mr. Beattie, to bind a match. After a lot of palaver, articles were eventually signed for us to run at Higginshaw Grounds, Oldham, on October 17th, distance 150 yards, Mills to allow me three yards' start. He was also to allow me £7 to defray expenses. Almost immediately I started my preparation, choosing Powderhall Grounds, Edinburgh, as my practising track. My preparation progressed very favourably, and, after I had been in training three weeks, I won a £15 handicap from scratch at Powderhall. I ran my trial for the Mills match at Hawkhill, doing half-a-yard inside evens all the way. Mills would, therefore, require to do three-and-a-half yards inside to dead-heat with me. Thus, on paper, it looked a good thing for me. I journeyed up to Oldham the day previous to the race, accompanied by Mr. Walters, and Jimmy Duckworth, my trainer. Mr. Walters, by the way, had a big interest in the affair. A couple of leg stretchers on the Higginshaw track on the Friday afternoon and Saturday morning soon removed any stiffness I might have contracted on the five hours' journey, and I toed the mark upon that occasion feeling as well and as confident as I ever did. Mills never gained an inch on me the whole way, and I eventually won by five or six yards, doing one yard outside evens all the way, or two yards inside (14-4-5), from my mark. My share of the gate-money amounted to nearly £70 upon that occasion, and altogether I netted about £100 by the whole transaction. The slowness of the time, comparatively speaking, is accounted for by the fact that we ran up Higginshaw and against a slight breeze. Shortly after this match, I issued a challenge to run any man in England, bar Harper, with one yard start in 150 yards. No takers appeared, however, and I had to wait for a match until Cross offered to run me 300 yards on level terms, provided we laid him or his backer £60 to £40.

———>·<———

CHAPTER XIII.

I Run Cross at Edinburgh.

My match with Cross was looked forward to with great interest by the sports-loving public of Auld Reekie, and as the match was to be decided on Powderhall, we made sure of a large gate. Herein, however, we were disappointed, and I have since learned that the fact of our charging 1s. for admission, instead of the usual and popular "tanner," accounted for the paucity of the attendance. The Edinburgh public evidently do not believe in paying 1s. to see one foot race, when at almost any time they can see a whole afternoon's foot-racing for sixpence. I still kept on training on Powderhall, while Cross, I believe, took his exercise on the Hawkhill track. As the 19th of December drew nearer, the crowd of spectators at our practice spins grew larger. About a fortnight before the 19th, we "dodged" the crowd, arriving at Powderhall about 1.30, when the ground was empty. These mysterious movements were merely for the purpose of running a trial in privacy. There were only about half-a-dozen people present, and all these belonged to our own party. My backers were well pleased with the result, but, unfortunately, the time leaked out, and the odds, which before had been six to four on me, rose to two to one on. A "downey" trick to get a better price was now attempted. It transpired that I was going to run a trial at a certain time one day. In consequence, there were about 30 or 40 people on the ground " seeking information." I gave my trial horse, W. Williams, 12 yards, and carrying three-quarters-of-a-pound of lead in either hand, was just beaten on the worsted. The time was a full second slower than in my genuine trial, and so well did the ruse succeed, that the odds went back to six to four on. At this price I was a firm favourite, and on the day of the race there was so much public money for me, that I eventually started at three to one on. The day was beautifully fine, though bitterly cold, and the ground was frozen as hard as a board. Cross won the toss, and naturally chose the inside. My orders were to "lie behind," and not attempt to get in front till the straight was reached. It went very much against the grain for me to do this, but when the pistol cracked, and Cross darted off at full speed, I made no attempt to pass him. At 200 yards we were together, and once in the straight I put my head down, and mentally ejaculating, "Good-bye, Billy," left him at every stride. Poor Billy had run himself practically to a standstill, and I came home by myself in 31 4-5secs. I did very poorly, financially, over this affair, but my reputation as a runner and a trier were considerably augmented by my victory.

CHAPTER XIV.

First Handicap at Powderhall.

The greatest pedestrian event of the year, the Powderhall New Year Handicap, of 1897, came off exactly a fortnight after my match with Cross, so it was not to be expected that I would be in very good sprinting form. Harper, the then champion, had to give me three yards in this event, but it was hardly likely that any importance would be attached to our meeting, if indeed we should meet.

I was backed to win a small sum, somewhere between £300 and £400, by my own party, and one enthusiast (not in our school, by the way) took £100 to £3 about my chance. I won my heat, but was beaten in the second round by Burns, of Glasgow (13), who, however, could only manage to get fourth in the final. I was not destined to come from that meeting without adding to my list of professional successes, for I won the 300 "hands down," off the five yards mark. I might add—it can do me no harm now—that I could have won it off scratch. About a week after this event, Bredin and I signed articles to run 400 yards for £50 a side, on a ground to be mutually decided upon. The Bolton track was eventually selected. I went into training, partly at Powderhall, and partly at Hawkhill. I was living at the Granton Hotel, near Edinburgh, at the time, and both grounds are very easy to reach therefrom, the journey by rail only occupying a few minutes.

I remember that the weather during my course of training was simply abominable. Nearly every morning the track would be covered with snow, which had to be swept off before I could run. Sometimes a thaw would come, and then I had the pleasure of running over my ankles in slush. I arrived in Bolton, accompanied by Bill Harvey (who was training me), and a friend, Mr. Shankland, of Granton Hotel. Mr. Shankland was putting down half the stake money for this affair, while I was finding the other half. Harvey put up at the Saddle Hotel, while Mr. Shankland and myself were entertained by some friends in the Chorley New-road, Bolton. The track was in a frightful state with half-melted snow, and scarcely fit to run on, but a gang of men, working night and day, got it into something like condition before the time arranged for the start. Bredin won the toss, but chose the outside, philosophically remarking that I would soon have the inside at any rate. He was not far wrong, as I was leading by three yards in the first ten. I rattled off the first 300 yards in 32 seconds, Bredin following six yards behind, but running full of power with that long, sweeping stride that never seems to tire. I was beginning to have enough of it before the straight was reached, but heaved a sigh of relief when I recollected that it was only 40 yards from the last corner to the worsted. I struggled home about two yards in front, "beat" to the world. I got to the "stripping box" somehow, and after an hour or so felt none the worse. The time was 44 4-5, which, considering the state of the track, speaks for itself.

CHAPTER XV.

THE NEWCASTLE SWEEPSTAKES.

IT was a small, but jovial party, that returned to Edinburgh from Bolton. Many witticisms were made, and the company were not particular whether the jokes were old or new, good or bad, but laughed at each fresh sally. A soldier on furlough entered our compartment at Preston, and from him, amid shrieks of laughter, I purchased a small fox-terrier; at least, he said it was a fox-terrier, and I took his word for it. At Preston, the unlucky beast was christened (with beer) "Edgar Chichester," the Bolton Wanderer. This euphonious title was shortened to Jack eventually. Jack was not a success. He possessed a pair of front legs which forcibly reminded one of those of a Chippendale table, wherein he differed greatly from his illustrious namesake.

I tried very hard to keep in training after my race with Bredin, and for three days stuck in like a veritable Trojan. In reality, however, I was sick of training, so, as the poet has it, I gave it up, and proceeded to enjoy myself. My chances for the Newcastle Sweepstakes, which came off ten days after the Bredin match, were by no means enhanced by my methods of enjoyment. In fact, when I ran a trial two days before the sweepstakes, I could only do two-and-a-half yards worse than evens, otherwise known as "quarter second." I was so disgusted with myself, that I determined to run another trial. I did so after a quarter-of-an-hour's rest. This time I ran half-a-yard slower. I went to a dinner that evening, thereafter spent an hour at a theatre, and wound up at a dance, at which I remained till 2.30, arriving home about 3 a.m. The cabman who drove me to my domicile sarcastically remarked that "if folks carried on like that they couldn't expect to be backit by other folk." He further remarked that "he wasn't going to jeopardise his hard-earned money." I advised him not to very strongly, taking care to impress upon him at the same time that I was keeping my money in my pocket, as far as the event referred to was concerned. He left me on the doorstep eventually, and drove off, muttering that in his belief "some folks was daft."

As was to be expected, I was very stiff next day, and though we had arranged to have a run at Powderhall in the forenoon, I pleaded pains all over, and we gave Powderhall a miss. We landed at Newcastle about 5.30 that afternoon, and passed the evening enjoyably enough at a theatre. I turned out on the track in the morning, and found, to my great joy, that my stiffness had completely vanished. After my morning run we had dinner, and then I went to bed. The sweepstake was advertised to take place between the second round and final of a second-class handicap, and was divided into two heats, of which Wilkinson (2¼), Redshaw (2¾), and myself (1¾), comprised the first, and Harper (scratch), Bannister (4), and Bridle (3¾), the second. Just before we retired to the dressing-room, Harper asked me to join him in boycotting the sweepstake, as he had good information to the effect that Bridle had the sweep at his mercy. I thought for a second or two, and then decided to run, be Bridle who he may. In my heat I had the greatest difficulty in giving Wilkinson his start; indeed, it was only in the last stride that I caught him, with Redshaw an inch or two behind. Harper did not turn out in the second heat, and Bridle had an easy victory over Bannister.

I wasted no time after the decision of the heats, but jumped, half-dressed, into a cab, and made straight for my bed at the hotel for an hour's rest. Just as I was thinking of getting up, I remembered that a glass of old port had once put some speed into me on a similar occasion in my amateur days. Bill Harvey, accordingly, brought me a tumbler half full. "Here," he said, "have a drop o' this." I took the lot! I felt, as soon as the generous liquid was stowed away, that I could run for a kingdom. When we got back to the track, the fielders were shouting "4 to 1 Downer." I thought, "Well, if odds count for anything, I'm beat now;" but, then, that kindly old wine kept murmuring, "Never mind the odds; get down to it." Very little time was wasted once we were stripped, and old Jimmy Young got us away to a perfect start. At 80 yards I was level with Bridle, and then drew clear away from him, winning in four yards faster time than I had done in my heat. During the whole ten years that I have been running, I never saw such enthusiasm displayed over a foot race. The palings just past the worsted collapsed with the crush behind, and the spectators, who were lining the barriers about 20 deep just at that spot, fell pell-mell over each other. One grimy collier was so overcome with excitement, that he embraced me, and, not satisfied with that, he must needs impress a kiss, anything but fairy-like, upon my damask cheek. The police had to come to the rescue and make a lane through the crowd, to enable me to get to the dressing-room. A huge mob, however, waited and accompanied me to the cab we had in readiness, but we managed eventually to drive off to the hotel amid peace.

My share of the stake came to £90, but I was only backed to win a very small amount, my bad trial having dispelled any hopes my party may have had of my winning.

I went up to London that night, partly for pleasure, and partly to arrange details with Bredin as to a quarter-mile match to which he had challenged me, and which I had accepted a few days before the sweepstakes.

———>·<———

CHAPTER XVI.

I Meet Bredin at a Quarter.

I DID not meet Bredin in London, but his friend, Mr. Lloyd Roberts, turned up in his stead. After the usual finessing and talk, articles were signed for us to run 440 yards for the Championship of the World (Bredin had previously beaten Mills for the honour) and £100 a side, on a ground and date to be mutually agreed upon, and failing a selection being made within one month, the stakeholders were to appoint the same. Talking about signing articles, reminds me of a funny incident that occurred during this process for my match with Mills. William Mills is very fond of the sound of his own voice, and is never so happy as when he has the chance of talking. Upon this occasion ample scope was afforded "Billy" for the display of his conversational powers, and after having had the floor to himself for about half-an-hour, the paper was pushed across for him to sign. This he did in most laborious fashion, and at length his signature was attached to the agreement. My turn came next, "Billy" watching the proceedings with interest.

"Tha' may be a better scholar than me, owd lad," he remarked, "but ahm best runner."

"I don't know, 'Billy,'" ventured a bystander; "you ought to be an orator."

"I know nowt about orator," replied "Billy," "Ahm champion of England, if that's what tha' means."

But to return to our match. Bredin and I eventually decided to run upon the Rochdale track on May 1st, 1897 and both went into training immediately. I had a week's rest in Edinburgh, and then with Jimmy Duckworth hied me South to Ormskirk on the 1st March. Some time previous to this, however, I had signed articles with " Billy " Cross to give him three yards' start in 150 for £50 a side, and to run at West End Grounds, Wigan, on the 20th March. Hence I had only three weeks to get fit, and so without any more to do I buckled down, and came on so well that my trial, run the usual two days before the race, dispelled all doubts as to my eventually winning.

I had a big party of friends from all parts staying at Ormskirk, and the journey to Wigan was quite a pilgrimage, though the tales with which we beguiled the journey did not resemble those of Chaucer's heroes. As our party expected, I won very easily, but as I started at four to one on, we literally had to buy money. Considerable interest and excitement were manifested over this race, as Cross was a favourite in Lancashire, and the public were keen to see him run. The time, I may mention, was considerably inside evens, and I think I can dismiss this race with the remark that, owing to the wretched accommodation and arrangements, a considerably larger crowd saw the race free than by paying.

Coming back to the Bredin race. I took a run up to Edinburgh after the Cross affair for a couple of days, eventually settling down to work at Ormskirk a good five weeks before the race. Try as I liked, I could not get the distance at any speed. One day I bethought me that exercise upon a punch-ball might supply the much-felt want, and accordingly I had a ball sent from Edinburgh. When one is in training for a distance like 440 yards, one wants to do a lot more work than when training for a sprint. The work, too, must vary, for, if one does nothing but run, run,

run, staleness very soon sets in, and that, probably, before one is in anything like condition. Hence the introduction of the punch-ball into my system of training; of course, I would try no experiments of this sort without first consulting Duckworth. Upon my suggestion that we should try ball-punching as a means of obtaining staying power, that worthy replied, "the very thing," and it was. I soon experienced no difficulty in getting the distance at something like a respectable pace.

I had a lot of friends staying in Ormskirk at that time, and the whole business was like a jolly picnic. True, there were times when the others went off for a jaunt to Liverpool or Manchester, and I would wish for a moment that I were not in training. This very seldom happened, however, for I liked my work, and it was very rarely that I experienced any desire to return to the flesh-pots of Egypt.

One fact in connection with this preparation astounded both Jimmy Duckworth and myself. I got to sprint very fast. As a rule, training for distances over 300 yards tends to reduce a man's speed, while it develops his staying power. My stride, too, increased in length—not that this is of any material advantage, but I only mention it as a fact that may prove interesting.

I know a rather funny anecdote about the length of a man's stride, which runs as follows: A certain collier was backed to run a match with another grimy gentleman. He was sent to undergo a preparation, and, as usual, had to run a trial on the watch. His time showed that he had little or no chance against his adversary, and his backers decided to let him run unbacked. Upon learning their decision, our collier shouted: "To blazes wi' watch, measure stride." This was done, and his party found, to their great glee, that he was striding two or three inches further each stride than in his former trial, and decided to back him forthwith. After the race, in which our friend was most ignominiously beaten, he remarked, ingenuously, "that he was striding far enough, but he didn't think he picked 'em up fast enough."

But, in the words of the shilling shocker, this is a digression. As I said before, I improved upon my sprinting in the most marvellous fashion, so much so, in fact, that I persuaded my backers (Messrs. Gibson and Shankland) to allow me to accept in the "Broughton Rangers' Sweepstakes," which was to be run on Good Friday, a fortnight and a day before I was due to run Bredin. I ran a trial for this event, and showed running which, provided I could reproduce it, left no doubt in our minds as to the winner. The good luck with which I seemed to be blessed at that time, however, temporarily deserted me, and in this manner. Everybody knows what an awkward day Good Friday is to travel on. All our arrangements were nicely made beforehand. We were to catch a certain train at Ormskirk and another at Rainford Junction, which would land us in Manchester in nice time for me to have a run, and the whole party to have some lunch, while I could get a couple of hours in bed thereafter. "The best laid plans of men and mice," however, "aft gang agley," and our disgust at learning that the train, owing to a breakdown, was three-quarters-of-an-hour late, can be imagined. This was bad enough, but when we got to Rainford and found that we had lost the connection, and that there was no train for four hours, I leave the reader to imagine our despair—and language. A kindly porter, who seemed to be the only intelligent creature in that benighted spot, suggested that we should drive to Wigan, distance seven miles, and there we should probably be able to get a train to take us to Manchester in time for the handicap. Anything was better than waiting in a dismal hole like Rainford, and accordingly two of the party set out to look for a conveyance. In about an hour, which time the rest of us spent in playing "Tip-it" in a little public which smelt horribly of candle grease, they returned with a waggonette which had seen many summers, and appeared to be on its last legs, as, indeed, did the animal harnessed thereunto, which, our emissaries said, they were told was a horse. This antediluvian structure was intended to hold five, and there were eight of us, with luggage. I don't like to think about that journey ; to make matters worse, it rained the whole two hours which we took to accomplish the seven miles. Twice the crowd had to get out of the crazy old conveyance and help the wheezy old bag of bones to extricate it from a rut. All things come to an end sooner or later, and this journey to Wigan was no exception, although it was a miserably wet and dejected looking crew that entered the Victoria Hotel that memorable Good Friday in quest of dinner and sundry hot drinks. While dinner was preparing, Duckworth and I paid a visit to the West End Grounds, where I tried to run the stiffness out of my legs. The attempt proved anything but successful, and in a very melancholy mood, and with many railings against fortune, we returned to the hotel. We were lucky to get a train from Wigan at two o'clock ; but as the sweep was advertised for 3.30, we had very little time to spare. We put up for the afternoon at "Sonny" Morton's, then in Chapel Street, Salford, and I went straight to bed upon our arrival. Only half-an-hour's rest was allowed me, and I was rubbed down and hustled on to the ground in double quick time.

Four other competitors toed the mark upon that occasion, and they were : Harper, on scratch ; Shepherd, of Rochdale, $5\frac{1}{2}$; Hardman, of Manchester, 8 ; and Briggs, of Pendleton, 9. My mark was $1\frac{1}{2}$. I may be wrong as to the exact starts, but as I am writing from memory, my readers will pardon me if I am in error. After the usual delay at the mark, Hepplethwaite took us in hand, and we were despatched to a magnificent start. It was soon evident that Hardman was going to win, which he eventually did by three-quarters-of-a-yard, with Shepherd and myself deadheating for second place. Harper was fourth, while Briggs brought up the rear. The dead-heat between Shepherd and myself occasioned a lot of talk, and, indeed, a match was made a few weeks later, but of that anon. It is always my rule (I say "is," for my running days, I trust, are by no means over), once a race has been run, to bother no more about it, but to look out for "fresh woods and pastures new." I could not, however, help indulging in a little self-commiseration upon this occasion. It was such hard lines. I had not run up to my trial by two yards. Of course, my adventures in the early part of the day had knocked all the running out of me. All the same, Hardman ran a great race, and fully deserved his victory. I did not return to Ormskirk that night, for the Bolton Wanderers were holding a professional meeting the following day, as well as on the Monday afternoon. I therefore stayed over the week-end with some friends in Bolton. I did not greatly distinguish myself at Burnden Park, as the starts I was called upon to give away were beyond all limits of common sense. The Saturday meeting, by the way, was postponed for a week, and so I had to again break training, and this time only a week before the quarter-mile match with Bredin. The morning of the 1st of May found me as lively as a cricket, and, with my usual crowd of followers, I arrived at Rochdale about midday. Before lunch I had a walk up to the track, but as I had my matutinal spin before leaving Ormskirk, I did not strip, but contented myself with a walk round the track.

We had great difficulty, Duckworth and I, in securing a cab to take us to the grounds. After a long delay, however, we managed to get a hansom, and amid the benedictions of the staff of the "Albion," off we drove, and a few minutes after four I landed on the ground, where I met with a magnificent reception from the vast crowd (somewhere about 10,000, I believe). A more enthusiastic lot of spectators would be hard to find, and my worthy opponent and myself were cheered again and again as we took the customary walk round the track. Bredin won the toss, and chose the inside berth. A photographer "took" the pair on the mark; he wanted us to pose a second time, but to this I objected, as there was a keen east wind blowing, and running things are constructed with an idea to lightness rather than warmth. Hepplethwaite, as usual, operated with the pistol, and at the report I dashed away to the front, adopting the same tactics as at Bolton. At 300 yards I was about four yards in front, and then Bredin began to draw closer, reaching my shoulder just as we reached the straight, which at Rochdale is about 60 yards in length. This was as near as he got, however, for amid a mighty roar from the crowd I let loose what remaining strength I had, and gradually widened the gap between us, finally breaking the worsted about four yards in front. The scene at the finish baffles description. I myself was unconscious of what was happening, having fainted dead off, but I was told that I was in danger of being suffocated by the crowd, who rushed across the grass in thousands. However, even an enthusiastic crowd, albeit a Rochdale one, cannot exist for ever, and after an hour or so we were able to get back to the hotel. I made about £240 by this match, £168 of which was realised by my share of the gate, which came to £400 before expenses were deducted.

CHAPTER XVII.

A Holiday at Professional Meetings.

As might be expected, I was in great demand that summer as a draw at pedestrian gatherings. Among these were those of the Cardiff Hibernian Society, Jarrow, the Glasgow Merchants' Cycling Club, West of Scotland Harriers, Bowness-in-Windermere, Galashiels, and others.

The first meeting I ran at after my quarter-mile victory was at Jarrow. I did nothing, however, as the starts were far too long. How is it that handicappers cannot realise that even a scratch man's speed has its limit ?

Two days after this, however, came the " Glasgow Merchants' " Sports, and thereby hangs a tale. While in training for the " 440 v. Bredin," I had some correspondence with the secretary. His committee wanted me to arrange a match to be run there, but I suggested that a handicap, say at 220 yards, would take much better. This was advertised accordingly, and a good entry was received. The competitors were divided into three heats, and the first and second in each heat qualified for the final. I ran nicely into second place in my heat, if my memory does not deceive me, reserving my strength for the harder tussle in the final. The other finalists sent Bill Harvey, who was looking after me for the time being, to ask me if I would divide the prize-money among the lot, provided they let me win for the sake of my name. This I declined to do, telling Harvey to let them understand that they were welcome to what prize-money they won, " but I would save a dollar all round· " if they were agreeable. I may mention that the "saving of a dollar all round" is a customary practice in the final heat of all small handicaps. It is not compulsory, but I have very seldom seen any man decline to do so when asked. It merely means that the winner will give each of the other finalists five shillings. Upon this occasion the other finalists declined to "save," and I knew that I would have to look out for squalls. And squalls there were, sure enough ! One man attempted to stop dead in front of me, but I was too wary for him, and slipped past him on the inside. Three others spread themselves over the track in such a manner as to force me right to the outside, attempting to make me stop. Even then, however, they were sold, for I ran on to the cement track, which lies outside the other, and along it for 20 or 30 yards, then on to the cinders when I had passed the others, finally winning by a yard or two. I was, naturally, furious at the manner in which the others had treated me, and told them what I thought of them.

However, the management showed their appreciation of my efforts in a very tangible and highly satisfactory manner, so that I had no cause to grumble. At Cardiff, where I was also well paid, I ran second in the 300, which was won in very fast time. Bredin ran second in the Quarter on the same occasion ; both these races were handicaps. A most amusing incident happened at one of my engagements that summer. I was asked to give an exhibition at some sports which were to be held under the laws of the A.A.A., and for which they offered to pay me well. I consented, but while I was on the ground, however, a wire came, addressed to the secretary, and which ran, "Downer must not be allowed to run. Stop the race at all hazards," and signed by the secretary of the S.A.A.A. The sports secretary came up with the missive in a great state, and asked me what was to be done. I told him I would have to be paid my fee, whatever happened ; that was all I had to do in the matter.

I was allowed to run. I met the secretary of the S.A.A.A. that same evening, and he waxed exceedingly wroth ; said that I would be the cause of not only the club, but of all the competitors at the sports, being suspended. I merely ejaculated, "Hurray !" That summer—the happiest I ever spent—came to an end all too soon for me. At Bowness-in-Windermere, I "broke down," and only two days before I was to run Bredin 440 for a purse of £110, offered by the West of Scotland Harriers. Stopping the race at Glasgow was out of the question, so a medical friend and I "faked" the leg up with bandages as best we could. Luckily, I was in very good health at the time, so the loss of a bit of practice the day before the race, and on the morning thereof, did not affect me much.

Bredin gave me the inside position, though I wanted to toss for it, and, following my usual tactics, I darted off at a good pace. For the first 100 yards my leg felt all right, and I was beginning to flatter myself that, although I might not win, yet I would be able to make a good show. Very soon, however, I began to feel the muscle giving way, and my speed began to relax. At about 200 yards Bredin drew level, and, although I made frantic efforts to regain the lead, I was forced by sheer pain to desist from the struggle, and at about 250 yards I dropped on to the grass. Then there was a scene ; shouts of "barney," "sell," and hisses and hoots were uttered by the most ignorant crowd of spectators it has ever been my bad luck to run before. A certain Glasgow paper, which professes to be an authority on athletics, strove to be very witty at my expense. They ventured a step too far, however, and a threat of an action for libel brought the proprietors to their senses, and an apology into the columns of an early issue of their paper. This apology was inserted word for word as my counsel composed it.

Before the *fiasco* at Glasgow, I had signed articles to run Bradley 100 yards on level terms for £100 a side, and to run Shepherd off our respective marks in the "Broughton Rangers'" Sweepstakes. When I broke down, I had £20 down for Shepherd's match, and £25 for Bradley's. I took a week's rest at Southport immediately after the Glasgow 440, and then, feeling much better, I persuaded my backers to post the £10 deposit which was then due for the Shepherd match. After another week at Southport, I felt sufficiently well to resume training, and accordingly departed for Edinburgh (I had selected the Granton Hotel as my training quarters) on Friday, June 25th, which allowed me three clear weeks in which to get fit for the Shepherd match. For the first three days I detected nothing wrong with my injured leg, but on the fourth it gave way in practice in such a manner as to assure me of my inability to compete against Shepherd on the date agreed upon, or even to don my pumps for several weeks. Thus my party had to lose £55, forfeited to Bradley and Shepherd, while I had to throw up several lucrative engagements.

My friends advised me to take a sea voyage as the best means of resting my wounded limb. I followed their advice, and selected Jamaica as being the most suitable place to visit in many ways. Accordingly, I sailed from Southampton on July 14th, 1897, and arrived at Kingston, Jamaica, on August 1st. Sea voyages are very much the same all the world over, chiefly, I presume, owing to the similarity of the surroundings, and this one did not differ from the general rule.

I spent the first few days of my visit in Jamaica enjoyably enough, visiting my friends and relatives, and as my "fame," such as twas, had preceded me, I had, on the whole, a very good time. I was not long in the island, however, before I contracted an attack of malarial fever, and it was thought advisable for me to curtail my visit and go home as soon as possible. I therefore departed by the next mail, arriving at Southampton on the 1st of September, and at Edinburgh on the following morning.

———>·<———

Wade, Photo.] [Edinburgh.
JOE GIBSON, ESQ., EDINBURGH.
Supporter of A. R. Downer.

CHAPTER XVIII.

"The Greatest Race I ever Ran."

Shortly after my return to this country from Jamaica, I re-started training, and some three weeks afterwards won a heat in a small sprint handicap at Powderhall Grounds. I was very much out of condition, however, and was badly beaten in the second round. Mr. Joe Gibson had found a good novice, and it was decided that Jim Duckworth, the novice, and myself should go to Ormskirk to train for the New Year Handicap at Powderhall. Accordingly, we were all three soon settled at the Talbot Hotel in the town of gingerbread, and hard at work. Little by little I began to improve, till, from conceding the novice 9 yards' start in 125, I could give him 10 in 120. We used to have pistol practice in the afternoon, running 50, 60, or 75 yards, as we felt inclined. At first I could only give him $2\frac{1}{2}$ in 50, but before our preparation was over, I could give him $3\frac{1}{4}$ in that distance, $3\frac{3}{4}$ in 60, and $5\frac{1}{2}$ in 75. We ran a good many trials altogether, but two only are of note. One took place about three weeks before the handicap, and the other a week later. When the starts came out, it was found that the handicapper had docked the novice's start to the extent of two-yards-and-a-half. Even then, however, he appeared to have a good chance of winning.

In the first important trial, the novice was placed on the $11\frac{1}{2}$ yards mark (his start in the handicap was 13), while I ran off my right mark, viz., $1\frac{1}{2}$. I won the trial with a good half-yard to spare. We both ran well, and Mr. Gibson was delighted at the prospect of one or the other of us winning the handicap.

The last trial we had was exactly a fortnight before the race, and this time we ran as we had been handicapped. Mr. David Blair, a gentleman who has a great reputation in Edinburgh as a watch-holder, came to Ormskirk, on Mr. Gibson's behalf, to clock us. A terrific race resulted in the novice being just beaten, and Mr. Blair returned the time as $5\frac{1}{2}$ yards inside evens, making me do "4 inside" all the way. Now, as this time was $1\frac{1}{2}$ yards faster than the time in which the handicap had been won the year previous, it is not surprising that Mr. Gibson and Mr. Shankland should have backed me to the extent they did, viz., to win nearly £5,000. There was a lot of talk over what sceptics were pleased to term Mr. Gibson's foolishness, but if foolishness consists of taking 25 to 1 about a 6 to 4 chance, then I will admit that Mr. Gibson was guilty. People wondered why I had not accepted Harper's challenge to run on level terms, why I had not waited and got a match on with Bannister, etc., etc.

Why, the very fact of my making these matches would have published to the world at large that I possessed greater speed than I was given credit for, the one thing we were anxious to avoid. In sporting lingo, we decided to "go for the gloves;" to let all ideas of matches vanish, and go for the one big event.

The 1st of January, 1898, dawned a perfect day for a handicap, with scarcely a breath of wind. Our party turned up at the ground in good time, and we found that I had gone back in the betting to 33 to 1. This was owing to the fact that there was a lot of money coming for other competitors, chiefly Henderson, of Galashiels, and Duncan, of Langholm. The last bet made by one of our party was £100 to £3, taken by Mr. Shankland.

I got through my heat fairly easily, doing $3\frac{1}{2}$ inside evens all the way, but our novice was beaten by F. Sharpe, of

Edinburgh, who ran second in the final. The second day, on which the second round and final are always decided, was a repetition of the first. In my heat in the second round I was drawn with Duncan, of Langholm, 10½, and Frazer, of Sunderland, 7½ or 8, I forget which. We all got well away, and though I caught Frazer, and strained every muscle, nerve, and sinew to overtake Duncan, the latter won by a yard-and-a-half, in 12¼ sec., which made me do 4½ yards inside evens—a yard faster than was shown by my running on the first day, and half-a-yard faster than I had done in my trial.

Duncan won the final by two yards from Sharpe, who beat Henderson, of Galashiels, by a yard, and who in turn was half-a-yard in front of Wilkins, of Eckington (7½). This was the greatest race I ever ran, both as regards time, and the money I should have won had I been successful. There is no use crying over spilt milk, however, as Mr. Gibson said when condoling with me over the fact that my true form had been shown up to no purpose.

CHAPTER XIX.

My First Defeat in a Money Match.

After my unsuccessful attempt to win the big Edinburgh handicap, matters appeared to be at a standstill with me. I challenged "the world," from 100 yards to 440, but found no acceptors. Harper, who only six months before had offered me one-and-a-half yards' start in 130, could not now see his way to run me level. A fresh challenge, extended to 500 yards, brought out my old opponent, Bredin, and we signed articles to run 500 yards, for the championship of the world and £50 a side, on the Rochdale track on March 5th.

I decided to train at Edinburgh, and, consequently, started in real earnest about the last week in January, with Jimmy Duckworth, as usual, as my mentor. The Newcastle Sweepstake was run on the 5th February, exactly four weeks prior to the date of the Bredin affair. I again turned out, though with scant hope of success, for I had only been training for a fortnight, and for 500 yards. However, I ran very well, for though I finished last, I was only a yard behind the winner, E. Massey, of Ryhope. This time, there were four competitors, including Massey, Braithwaite ("Bridle"), and myself. We finished in the order named. The acceptance upon this occasion was £5, with £50 added by the promoters.

Upon my return from Newcastle, I found that I had contracted an attack of pleurisy, and then began a chapter of accidents. That pleurisy, slight though it was, was sufficient to keep me back for a week—a serious thing when

one has only a certain time in which to get fit. In spite of
this indisposition, however, I was able to turn out in the
Sheffield Shrovetide Handicap, for which Mr. Shankland
had entered A. Kinnear, of Newcastle. I ran a couple of
trials with Kinnear, the day before we left Edinburgh for
Sheffield, and he beat me by half-a-yard each time. The
handicap did not look a good thing on paper for either of
us, but where money is, money is to be had. We both won
our heats, but, while Kinnear got nicely home in the
second round, putting down the favourite, I "broke down"
just as I was getting nicely to the men. The breakdown,
this time, occurred to the ball of my right foot, and so
painful and swollen did it become, that we had to send for a
doctor. That worthy pronounced it gout, and gave me
some stuff wherewith to rub it, as well as a mixture for
internal use.

Kinnear won the handicap, and as I got about £17 out
of the handicap I did not do so badly, though I would have
forfeited three times that amount to have been spared the
misfortune which had befallen me.

I had decided to finish my training at Mr. Cairns' Red
Cross Hotel, Skerton, and Duckworth and I landed there at
four o'clock on the morning after the final of the Sheffield
Handicap, both in doleful dumps. The following morning
we set to work to doctor the sprained toe as well as we
could, but, in spite of hot water applications, rubbing, etc.,
we were finally compelled to resign all hope of running on
the 5th. Accordingly, on the Thursday, nine days before I
was to run Bredin, I despatched three telegrams, one to
Mr. Sharpe, the manager for the match, asking him to make
arrangements for postponement, one to Bredin, telling him
I was unable to run, and one to the *Sporting Chronicle*,
asking them to publish the fact abroad. Now, I should

mention, that I had had some correspondence with Bredin on the subject, the outcome of which was that he was agreeable to have the race postponed, provided that I paid the expenses of doing so. I agreed to this by letter, adding that I should wire as soon as I found I could not run. Hence my wire to him. I met Mr. Sharpe, at Preston, by appointment that evening (I was *en route* for Edinburgh), and we decided that the second Saturday in April would be the most suitable date for the match, as well as allowing me time to recover from my accident. In this, however, we were wrong, as subsequent events will prove. Mr. Sharpe promised to communicate with Bredin, and I continued my journey, which was for the purpose of arranging matters with Messrs. Gibson and Shankland, who were backing me. Immediately upon my arrival, I received a telegram from Bredin, in which he said he was unable to postpone the match. This was followed by a letter, which stated that, owing to having business in London which would occupy his time considerably during the next two or three months, the match would either have to be postponed indefinitely or else be run upon the date originally fixed. Here was a pretty "kettle of fish." Mr. Gibson, upon reading the letter, merely remarked, "I suppose we'll have to forfeit, and you can go to the infirmary." I thought for a moment, and then asked Mr. Gibson to stake up the £25 which was required to make up the full stake, and I would be good for it out of the gate money. There were two or three others present at the time of this conversation. "What!" said one, "you mean to run in a week, and you can hardly walk now! You must be mad."

"No," I replied, with a certain amount of jauntiness, "or if I am, there's method in my madness. I can hardly walk, that's true enough, but yesterday I couldn't walk at all; perhaps in a week I'll be able to raise a gallop." I then explained that if the match did not come off, I should be called upon to pay about £50 for expenses, which I could ill afford, while the gate money would be sure to more than recompense me for the £25 I was forced to speculate; besides, Mr. Gibson would now get a run for his money. This idea seemed the most satisfactory to all parties, and accordingly that night I returned to Lancaster, accompanied by Mr. Gibson and two friends. The others were as lively as possible, chiefly for my benefit, but my troubles were by no means over, for before we got to Carlisle I was seized with a violent fit of shivering, which always precedes an attack of malarial fever.

In my recent trip abroad I had contracted that malady, and am still subject to recurrences of it. We landed at Lancaster about two in the morning, and I was glad to get to bed. The next day I was so "seedy" that we sent for a doctor, who confirmed my fears regarding the fever. He told me that I would have to lie up for about a week, and, with a grave shake of the head, he doubted if I would be able to fulfil my engagement on the following Saturday. I laughed at this. "Why, doctor," I said, "if I have to be carried on to the track I'll have to run now, so patch me up as best you can." The following Wednesday, only three days before the match, I managed to get downstairs; the rest had done my foot good so far that I was now able to put it on the ground without pain, and could walk without limping.

The next day I got my pumps on and tried to run. To my surprise, I found that although I could not get on the toes of my right foot, yet by running on the flat of that member I could get along at a fair pace. I was dreadfully weak, however, and my friends were extremely anxious with regard to the issue of the race—not so far as the eventual winner was concerned ; that was a foregone conclusion, but as to what damage I might do to my internal economy by running so much out of condition. The day came at last ; never had pedestrian such a preparation ; and the whole party arrived in Rochdale overnight. We all went to the theatre that evening, after which to bed.

The next morning I contented myself with a walk round the track instead of participating in the customary spin. I arrived on the scene of battle a few minutes before the time. Bredin won the toss, and selected the inside berth, and to the crack of Hepplethwaite's pistol I went to the front, took the inside, and tried to get as far from my opponent as possible. At 200 yards Bredin came up to me, but I was not yet disposed of, however, for I immediately spurted and put a couple of yards between us. He soon made this up, and again tried to pass me. I again retaliated, but more feebly, and in a few seconds I had the mortification of seeing my opponent get in front and gradually draw away from me. A friend of mine rushed across the grass to me when we had about 150 yards to go, and Bredin would be about five yards in front. "Stick to him, Alf," he shouted ; "he's beat as well as you." I didn't think so, but I managed to struggle blindly into the straight, and got within 20 yards of the worsted just as Bredin was breaking it. How much further I should have run I do not know, but at this point Mr. Gibson ran on to the track and caught me, and thus I suffered my first defeat in a match for money.

CHAPTER XX.

AN ENFORCED REST.

AFTER the race described in the last chapter, I was advised to have my foot attended to at a Hydropathic. Following this advice, which coincided with my inclinations, I selected Smedley's, at Matlock, and the house doctor there told me that I was suffering from gout, thus bearing out his Sheffield brother's verdict. I was treated accordingly. I was told I must not eat this nor drink that; I must go to the baths three times a day, and there undergo a treatment which they prescribed for me.

Now, Matlock is one of the healthiest places in England, and after I had been there two or three days I began to feel extremely well, with a most voracious appetite. In fact, I got as fit as a fiddle, and only longed for a sound toe and a running track to feel my old self again. The latter was possible, but it seemed as though I were doomed to go "dot and carry one" for the rest of my natural existence; for, in spite of liver-packs and all the other propaganda prescribed in that establishment for the treatment of gout, my foot remained in much the same condition. It was a very happy life, nevertheless, and I enjoyed my stay there immensely, but, at the same time, it was not bringing in any grist to the mill. After three weeks, as my foot did not make any improvement, I began to get anxious. I had been recommended to consult Dr. Wharton Hood, the specialist, in London. This I did, and Dr. Hood examined my foot. Without a moment's hesitation he pronounced it to be nothing worse than a bad sprain, and told me that if

I followed his instructions I would soon be all right. He
sent me to a medical rubber, and for ten days I had my
unfortunate toe rubbed for half-an-hour at a sitting.
Thereafter Dr. Hood strapped it up for me, and at the
same time showed me how to do so for myself. Then he
dismissed me with his blessing. I had no chance for some
time of testing the efficacy of Dr. Hood's treatment, but I
made certain in my own mind that I was once more sound
in wind and limb. Although I had thoroughly thus convinced myself, yet I found it very difficult to get other
people of the same opinion, and for some time I was
"gafferless." At length, Harper and Bannister, who were
matched to run 120 yards on level terms, advertised their
match as being for the championship of the world. To
this I naturally objected, for, putting aside all other
reasons, the match came about through Bannister offering
to run any man in England "bar Downer." I published
my objection in the *Sporting Chronicle*, and Harper immediately replied to the effect that he was the champion, and
that I had only challenged the world hearing that he was a
bit off colour; but, provided he was successful against
Bannister, he would run me 130 yards for £200 a side.
Here was a chance at last. Harper beat Bannister, and
repeated his willingness to run me. I was not long in
finding a backer in the person of Mr. W. Craig, a well-known Edinburgh sportsman, who replied, on my behalf, that
Harper could be accommodated for as much money as he
could find up to £500; and a cheque for £25, to bind a
match, accompanied this reply. In spite of Harper's
challenge, however, no notice was taken of this deposit, and,
to my disgust, we did not meet.

HARRY HUTCHINS.
Winner of several Sheffield Handicaps.
The Fastest Sprinter of the Century.

CHAPTER XXI.

Matches against Hutchins, Keane, and Bredin.

I find that this story is becoming much longer than I intended. I shall, therefore, be compelled to cut short the account of the next two or three matches in which I took part. The first I had after recovering from my breakdown was against Harry Hutchins, the old champion and record holder, who offered to take seven yards' start in 200 from me for £25 a side. A friend of mine found the needful, and I went into training at Flamborough, where I soon got into something like form. A week before my match with Hutchins was decided, came the Sheffield Doncaster Handicap. In this I was beaten in the second round by T. F. Keane, of America, who had won the previous handicap, and who was in receipt of two-and-a-quarter yards from me. I found, to my intense disgust, that I was not nearly so fit as I ought to be, but I kept my own counsel about this. I beat Hutchins all right, though I only made 10s thereby. It happened thus :—

Hutchins, it seems, was working for two men, one of whom was finding the "stake" while the other found the "steak." The gentleman who was putting down the money complained that Hutchins was not treating him fairly in the matter of trials, or something of that sort, and withdrew his money from the *Chronicle* office. I was apprised of this the evening before the race by a telegram from the *Chronicle* people, who asked, at the same time, if the race was to go on. I replied to the effect that as all arrangements had been made and the ground engaged, the race would have to go on, and we would see about the stake afterwards. The race was run, and I got home by about a foot in 22 1-5sec. The gate money amounted to nearly £100, of which my share came to £29.

Shortly afterwards Keane and I signed articles to run 200 yards, Keane to have two-and-a-half yards inside the distance, for £50 a side. This race took place on the Rochdale track, round two corners, on October 22nd, 1898, and I again proved successful, my time being returned at sound 20sec. Although I started at four to one, and thereby created a big surprise by winning, I did very badly, financially, out of this affair, only getting some £30, which included my share of the "gate." The day was one of the worst I have ever seen, and although it stopped raining just prior to the match, yet we knew the gate was ruined. I was lucky at this time to find a backer in the person of a gentleman from Southport, who supported me to run Bredin 500 yards on level terms, for £50 a side. Bredin was agreeable, and we decided to run at Barrow-in-Furness, on December 26th. I trained for this event at Ormskirk, in company with A. Kinnear, the Sheffield handicap winner.

It proved a desperate race at Barrow, and Bredin, staying the better, won by a yard-and-a-half in 59sec. dead. I fell heavily on the track at the finish, skinning my elbow rather badly ; so badly, in fact, that blood poisoning set in about a fortnight afterwards. I ran at Edinburgh in the New Year handicaps, but did nothing, my effort at 500 having deprived me, for the time being, of my sprinting powers. Shortly afterwards, having recovered from the blood poisoning, I went into training for the Newcastle Sweepstake, which was to come off on February 25th. I chose Ormskirk as my training quarters, and my backer sent for

T. F. KEANE.

Winner of Three and 2nd in two of Five consecutive Sheffield Handicaps.

the celebrated Bill Bottomley, of Huddersfield, to put me through my paces. I was badly beaten at Newcastle, off the scratch mark, by Wilkins, of Eckington ($5\frac{1}{2}$), who defeated Nener (6) in the final by three-quarters-of-a-yard.

CHAPTER XXII.

Charles Harper Vanquished.

SHORTLY after the Newcastle Sweep of 1899, my backer told me that I had better get a match on with Bredin at 470. This was managed with little difficulty, as Bredin, after our last tussle at Barrow, had suggested a match at this distance. I don't much fancy running races over 300 yards. In fact, once when I was matched to run Bredin 500 yards, a friend remarked facetiously, " Why, the little beggar will never do it ; he generally takes a cab when he goes that distance."

Bredin and I decided to run our 470 yards match at Rochdale (poor old Rochdale) on May 6th, and the stake-money was to be £50 a side. This odd distance, it will be noted, exactly splits the difference between 440 and 500.

As we signed articles at the beginning of March, we had plenty of time in which to get fit, and I did not bother for a week or two about going into training. However, a challenge from Harper in the *Sporting Chronicle*, in which he offered to take two yards in 130, for £50 a side, and run in six weeks, brought me back into the paths of—well, into training quicker than I intended. I fixed up a match eventually with the Bullwell ped., as the sporting press terms my lengthy opponent, he agreeing to take one-and-a-half yards in 130.

We eventually decided to run at Higginshaw on April 22nd. Bill Bottomley was again engaged to train me, and we finally decided to train from the Albion Hotel, Rochdale. My work for this, the most important sprint match I had

Wolstenholme, Photo.] *[Blackpool.*

C. HARPER.
Ex-Champion Sprinter of the World.

hitherto made, progressed without a hitch. Bill Bottomley was attention itself, while Mr. and Mrs. Crabtree, of the Albion Hotel, could not do enough to make us both comfortable.

Of course, it looked, at first sight, a foolhardy thing to allow myself only a fortnight for an important match like the 470 against Bredin, after training for a sprint ; but, as Bill remarked, I would in any case do the same work if training for 440, only with, perhaps, a little more running round the ring during the last fortnight.

We got to Higginshaw on the day arranged in good time, and found that the betting was two to one on me, or seven to four Harper. Harper turned up a few minutes later, and we both retired to the dressing-room to strip. Little time was wasted once we were on the track again, and to a beautiful start Hepplethwaite sent us on our journey. I was soon at my opponent's shoulder, but from 60 to about 90 yards he kept his advantage. At about this point, however, I made a desperate effort, and drew level about 20 yards from home. It was all over now, and I eventually won by a good half-yard. The official time was returned at two-and-a-half yards inside evens, but other watches made it much faster, their times averaging about three-and-a-half inside. As I did this time in my trial, and I always (bar accidents) reproduce my trial form in the race, I am inclined to believe it.

I fancy that in this race I put my claim to be considered champion sprinter beyond all cavil.

I allowed myself no relaxation after the Harper match, but re-started training almost immediately for my 470 with Bredin. Everything went on all right until a week from the race, when I fell ill with quinsy—a nice state of matters, truly ! I had to keep in bed for two or three days, and was only allowed out on the Tuesday, when I made a feeble attempt to run. On the Wednesday I was a little better, though a trial over 400 yards on the Thursday proved that I was anything but myself, and would have little chance with Bredin at his best. We had learned, however, that that gentleman had strained his knee or some other portion of his anatomy, so chances seemed about equal.

The race was run on a beautifully sunshiny day, with a gale of wind blowing. Bredin, as usual, won the toss, and chose the inside. Our relative positions made very little difference, however, as I went to the front immediately, and at 120 yards was about ten yards ahead. As Bredin at this point did not seem to be gaining, I eased up, reserving my strength for the run in, which was against the wind. Bredin began to find some running about 200 yards from home, and to make up some leeway. I had gained too great an advantage, however, and won by two or three yards, in the slow time of 56secs. I was not a bit proud of this win, as Bredin was palpably unfit to run.

CHAPTER XXIII.

ON TRAINING : ADVICE TO YOUNG RUNNERS.

I HAVE often been asked to give an account of my methods of training. This is by no means a light task, as one cannot lay down a fixed rule and adhere to it. One must follow inclination to a certain extent, or very soon one gets utterly sick of the whole business.

For a sprint preparation one wants to feel as lively as possible when the work is to be done, and I do not think I can do better than give an account of the manner in which I trained for my match v. Harper in April, 1899. To begin with, I had five clear weeks in which to get fit, and as I can usually be depended upon to get into something like condition in three, I had thus two weeks to put on the finishing touches. Bill Bottomley, who trained me for this event, and myself arrived in Rochdale, where I had decided to train, on Saturday, March 18th.

The first two days I did little or no running, but contented myself with taking aperients, walking, ball punching, and dumb-bell exercise. On the Tuesday following our arrival I began business in real earnest, and as follows :—As a rule, I would run twice a day, the work varying according to circumstances. Generally, however, in the forenoon, I would have a couple of short runs of about 60 yards, starting slowly and gradually increasing my pace till I would be going at top speed, and letting my legs go of their own accord I would gradually ease up. These runs would be followed by what I call a " run through," which consists of going about 150 yards at medium pace, spurting the last 20 yards or so. Sometimes I would only "run through" about 120 yards, and at other times would even do as much as 200 yards. I have even substituted an easy, very easy, 300 yards or, upon two occasions only, 440 yards, for the other work.

I would then punch the ball for about two or three minutes, after which Bill would rub me down. I always used a platform ball, *i.e.*, one that you bang about suspended from a platform, as it admits of a greater variety of exercises than the "rubber top-and-bottom" ball. Ball-punching is, in my opinion, the finest thing in the world for the wind, besides saving the stress on the legs occasioned by running. My afternoon's work, except when I had a trial, would consist of two 60 yard dashes with the pistol. Sometimes I would have two 75's, or sometimes I would, in Bill's expressive phraseology, "play about a bit," and then go 100 yards once.

If I had a trial on in the afternoon, my morning's work would be very light, consisting, as a rule, of a couple of short runs without the pistols—"leg stretchers," in pedestrian parlance. I always used dumb-bells in the morning before I went for my walk, and I found that exercise highly efficacious in removing bed stiffness. Here is a time-table, which gives the daily routine which I followed for this preparation :—

```
a.m.                              p.m.
  8.0—Got up.                       2.0—Bed.
     Dumb-bells.                    3.0—Got up.
     Walk half-a-mile.                 Set out for ground.
  9.0—Breakfast.                       Ran.
 10.30-Set out for ground.          5.0—Tea.
     Ran.                           7.30—Walk two or three
     Punched ball.                      miles.
p.m.                                9.15—Supper.
  1.0—Dinner.                      10.30—Bed.
```

Wane, Photo.] [Edinburgh.

A. R. DOWNER.
Get on Your Mark.

Meals never trouble me at any time. So long as the cooking is good—and at the Albion, Rochdale, it is above reproach—I don't care what I eat. Chops, or bacon and eggs, followed by a little marmalade, used to form my breakfast. Dinner would consist of a cut off a joint, or some chicken, followed by a milk pudding, stewed fruit, etc.; while for tea I would have either fish, poached eggs, sweetbreads, or—in fact, anything light. I would only occasionally have supper, and then light, for a good night's rest is a most important factor in training.

Of course, this sort of preparation would not suit everybody; in fact, very few pedestrians like their pistol practice in the afternoon; but I must be built in a contrary mould, for I certainly prefer it, and, what is more important, thrive on it.

It is, moreover, not to be expected that all budding champions can be sent away for a five or six weeks' preparation. One must be very careful to avoid doing too much track work. Pistol practice, too, must not be indulged in too frequently, or that "*bete noir*" of the pedestrian—a breakdown—may ensue, and then farewell to training for weeks, or perhaps months. In fact, most trainers opine that a couple of shots per diem is amply sufficient.

Most athletes, amateurs especially, can only afford time to run once a day, in which case one pistol crack, followed by an easy canter of from 120 to 200 yards, is sufficient three days out of the six, two pistol cracks at about 60 being sufficient for the other three. Of course, the work must vary according to circumstances, and according to the man's strength. Some men, too, can stand, in fact, require, a lot more work than others. However, with the exercise of a little common sense, the runner can soon find out what suits him best, as well as his best distance. Dumb-bells should be used first thing in the morning. Cold baths are bad, as they stiffen the muscles, though when training for a "quarter" they may be taken, with less harm, two or three times a week. For my part, when I have been training for 440 or 500 yards, I have had a cold sponge down immediately upon getting out of bed. I found this very strengthening, although it had a great tendency to reduce my speed. It is, therefore, questionable whether any material advantage was gained thereby. By the way, the training required for a "quarter" should not greatly differ from the method employed in a sprint preparation; substitute an easy run over the distance twice (not oftener) a week for the other work, and I think the average runner will find that sufficient. And now a word of advice to young runners. Don't imagine, because you can beat a few of your friends, that you must be a flier. I am not one to throw cold water on anyone's endeavours, but over-confidence is as bad as a funk. There is only one way to run a sprint race, and that is, as fast as you can run in your own natural style, and if you should be getting beaten, don't throw your head back in desperation. Remember, a race is never lost till the worsted is broken, and you never know your luck. You may, for all you know, be a stronger finisher than the man you think is beating you.

As regards starting, I have tried nearly every style under the sun, and I find my present one by far the best. This is it. I have two holes made, each large enough to contain my toes comfortably. The first is about six inches from the line, while the other is about 20 inches behind the first. When the word is given to go to the mark, I place the left foot in the front hole, and the right in the other, with the ball of the left foot pressing firmly against the back of the hole, and place my right knee on the ground and my hands on the mark.

A. R. Downer.
Get Ready.

When told to get "set," or "ready," or whatever the starter's word may be, I raise my knee from the ground and assume an attitude like a cat about to spring. When the report rings out, I fly clean away from the holes, my right foot lands on the ground about four feet over the line, and in a second I am in full stride.

CHAPTER XXIV.

Notes on My Trainers.

I have had many trainers in my time, chief among whom may be reckoned "Jimmy" Duckworth, of Edinburgh. "Jim" understood me better than anyone else, myself included, and a knowledge of a man's temperament is half the battle to a trainer. We first became acquainted at the St. Bernard's Sports in 1892. I was on virtual scratch in the sprint handicap, and, having just won my heat, was looking for someone to rub me down prior to turning out in the second round. "Jim," whom I had never seen before, offered his services. "Thank you," I said, "you're a Christian." I also offered him a tip in the shape of a shilling. I was only an apprentice engineer, remember, and I had not as yet learned to turn my running abilities to account by the accumulation of wealth therefrom. "Na! na! my lad," he said; "you win the handicap, and that'll do me fine." The following summer, I put myself under Duckworth's charge, and he brought me on wonderfully. In fact, what confidence in my running I may be possessed of, I learned from old "Jim." He had a knack of talking to me about any race in which I might be running, which made me feel that it was impossible for me to get beaten, and that feeling I still have, except, of course, when I'm not fit. "Jim" trained me for all my Scotch championships, also for my matches with Mills, Cross, Bredin at 440, and for the first 500, in which, however, I was beaten, for the occasion upon which I showed four-and-a-half yards inside evens at Edinburgh, and for a host of minor events.

A. R. DOWNER
Beating Even Time.

He is terribly enthusiastic, and if he takes a fancy to the man he is training, he will work like a nigger to get him fit.

Bill Bottomley trained me for the Newcastle Sweep of 1899, for my matches against Harper and Bredin at 470, and also for the exhibition race at Cardiff, where I ran 350 yards in 36 1-5 sec., one of my best performances.

"Bill" is a most conscientious trainer, the very man to bring out a novice. He is very quick to discover a man's weaknesses, and is about the best judge of character I know. It seems rather strange that the man who trained Bradley for so many of his races with me should eventually become the trainer of his antagonist.

Other men who have looked after me in training are Bill Harvey, who helped me to get fit for my match with Bredin at 400, also for the Newcastle Sweep of 1897, which I won : "Shirt" Cook, who looked after me for a few weeks when I was an amateur ; and Kinnear, of Newcastle, who was with me when I ran Keane 200 yards, and Bredin 500 for the second time.

PART II.

CHAPTER I.

EDGAR CHICHESTER BREDIN.

E. C. BREDIN was born in Gibraltar in the year 1867, and was destined to become one of the most famous middle-distance runners of the century.

His career has been a very varied one, both in his private and pedestrian life. As an amateur, he secured races from 250 yards to 1,000 yards, and championship honours for both the quarter and half-mile, the former twice, and the latter three times. Later, in the professional world, he secured, the first time of asking, the world's championship at half-a-mile, which he successfully defended and retained against all comers, till in an evil moment Harry Cullum, of Cardiff, in the terribly slow time of 60 seconds, defeated him, not only for a considerable stake, but the much-coveted title of the half-mile champion. Again, in a private capacity, have we not heard of him, tea planting out in Ceylon; and again, doing the duties of an out-rider in the Mounted Police of the States or Canada, in company of a couple of kindred spirits. These three, by the way, issued a challenge to back a man at billiards, at fighting (weight for weight), and at running any distance from 250 yards to half-a-mile. But this is, perhaps, a digression. We must refer to just a few of his chief matches, simply saying, by the way, that Bredin has secured as many first honours as any pedestrian ever known.

E. C. BREDIN.
Half-mile Champion of the World.

On page 102, paragraph two, line nine—60 seconds should read *two minutes*.

Having commenced his career by meeting and defeating most of the big men in his own immediate district, we find him becoming a member of that—once, at all events—celebrated body, the London Athletic Club, making the foundation of a great name in the pedestrian world. In the year 1893, he won both the quarter and half mile championships of England, in the one afternoon, at the English Amateur Athletic Meeting. The quarter-mile was won in the splendid amateur time of $49\frac{1}{5}$ secs., and in the history of this English championship this time has only twice been beaten: once by that wonderfully versatile runner, L. E. Myers, of America (whose death all true lovers of pedestrianism mourned only a few months ago), and again by that splendid amateur, H. C. L. Tindall, who, next to Bredin himself, ranks as the best quarter and half-mile amateur champion we have ever seen. The half-mile was even a better performance than the quarter-mile, as his time, 1 min. $55\frac{1}{5}$ sec., not only ranks as the amateur record for the distance, but is the best he himself has ever done, either as an amateur or professional. This double event he was able to pull off in the following year, 1894, his time, though rather slower, ranking quite among the best recorded in these competitions. It should be further stated that Bredin again won the half-mile championship in 1895, this year running the distance in 1 min. $55\frac{4}{5}$ secs., and establishing a very good second to his own record of two years previously ; as a matter of fact, the time was only $\frac{3}{5}$ of a second slower. Having conquered and re-conquered all who came in competition with him, and being aware that some nice little "plums" were being picked by a number of athletic gentlemen, who had somehow run foul of that august body the Amateur Athletic Association, he very wisely decided that he would endeavour to partake of some share of the aforementioned "plums," hence we find him launched into the professional athletic world. His first important match was that against that wonder of the century, A. R. Downer, the Jamaica-Scot, the distance being 400 yards, and the venue, the track of the Bolton Wanderers' Football Club. Alas, and lack a day, he had found a "tartar." The Edinboro' gentleman not only defeated him, but established a world's record for the distance, namely, $44\frac{4}{5}$ secs.

Not to be denied, however, he cast a bait, by challenging his victor to a match, at 440, this being the distance at which (and up to the half-mile) he was the world's acknowledged champion. The pedestrian world wondered what the little Scotchman would say to this, as he was "all out" at 400 yards, and great was the surprise when he modestly covered the deposit. Articles were signed, the ground selected was that of the Rochdale Athletic Club, and the date, May 1st, 1897; and never will that day be forgotten by any who had the good fortune to see the race. Twelve thousand spectators from all parts of Great Britain, including almost every known man in both the amateur and professional world, were there, and the excitement baffles description—12,000 people, to see a race that would not last 50 seconds. With the majority, Bredin was established a strong favourite, as they thought that his opponent could not live the last 40 yards. The men got away well together, Downer using his superior speed to get in front, which he did at ten yards; for the next 100 yards, he increased his lead to two-and-a-half yards; at 200 yards, he led by four yards; at 300, Bredin began to creep up to his man, at 350, was with him, and ran shoulder to shoulder for the next 20, into the straight; Bredin was on the outside, and to use his own words, "just as I was about to make an effort to go in and win, Downer shot away from me, and bowled me out by six or seven yards"; the time was 49 $\frac{4}{5}$ secs. Bredin was thus deprived of the honour of the quarter-mile championship. He, however, got his revenge by twice defeating Downer over 500 yards. The memorable race at Barrow on Boxing Day, 1899, was as grand a race as the 440 at Rochdale, on May 1st, 1897, the result, however, being in Bredin's favour, Downer falling on the tape, beaten by half-a-yard, time being 59 seconds. For the half-mile championship, Bredin met and defeated the great Yankee Kirkpatrick, in 1897, and also defeated G. B. Tincler, 1899, but the race is described elsewhere in these pages. He, however, has had to surrender his long held claim and title to the half-mile championship. For after meeting and being defeated by H. Cullum, the Welsh champion, in a match at 1,000 yards, the latter accepted Bredin's challenge at half-a-mile, and at Rochdale on November 4th, 1899, again won the match, and this time the half-mile championship, but in the miserably slow time of 2 mins.

How this result came about, I am at a loss to understand, as Bredin had run the distance only three days before on a much slower track, in the good time of 1min. 57secs. So, for once in a way, an undisputed master of the art of pace was at fault.

The following are Bredin's ideas on training, and they should prove a great help to all tyros, both amateur and professional.

CHAPTER II.

Training Notes by E. C. Bredin.

In the matter of training, it depends a great deal whether one has business to attend to, or the whole day at his disposal, as is generally the case with professional athletes. The advantage is not altogether with the latter on this account, as the enforced rest and regular hours that have to be observed by the ordinary amateur are really beneficial in his training, and prevents a man from over doing his work, a fault which is very easy to fall into when all one's time is devoted to getting fit without the assistance of a competent trainer; nevertheless, I trust the following ideas on training for middle distances may be of use to young athletes of either class.

To begin the day, a little fresh air before breakfast is advisable, and the best way to obtain the same is by a short walk, should the weather be fine. After this meal, two hours should elapse before taking any violent exertion, and then follows a start to the track. Should the distance be short, walk four laps before donning the pumps, when, if training for distances such as 500, 600, 880, or 1,000 yards, it is advisable to commence by running 60 or 70 yards three or four times fast right through, with some minutes' interval between each burst. A companion during sprinting is a great aid; in fact, it is scarcely possible to run one's fastest at these short distances when running alone. The sprinting over, a rest of some quarter-of-an-hour to quite recover one's breath, or really to allow the heart time to get back to its normal state, and then some longer distance should be gone through, varying the same each day. For instance, on Monday, three-quarters of a mile ; Tuesday, 220 yards fast ; Wednesday, 600 yards ; and Thursday, 300 yards fast, it being always borne in mind that when running any distance over 300 yards in practice it is best to go well within oneself, and to make a point of finishing the last 70 yards or so as fast as possible.

After the mid-day meal, it is advisable to lie down for an hour's nap, or a quiet read, if disinclined to sleep. About three o'clock in the afternoon or later, should the weather be very warm, a walk of six or seven miles at a good pace, say each mile in 13 minutes, should end the day's work, with the exception of a stroll before going to bed, which is most advisable, specially during the winter months, when many evening hours have to be passed in a warm room. To a man inclined to put on flesh, a little sweating exercise, in addition to the above, could be taken with advantage about twice a week, and the best method in fine weather is to walk round the track for an hour well enveloped in sweaters and heavy clothing ; rubber shoes are good covering in such cases for the feet; on the other hand, should the weather be wet, skipping indoors, with a similar amount of clothing, is good exercise for the muscles all round, and a good way to get superfluous weight removed.

I do not believe a man training for the distance I am referring to requires to run twice daily ; for sprinting, this may be advisable, but I have a great opinion of the afternoon's walking exercise as a means to acquire health and strength. Some people prefer running in the afternoon, but if one gets through a great deal of work during the day, one is apt to get on the track slightly tired, in which case it is questionable whether much benefit is derived from a run, and a golden rule should be that if one feels totally disinclined to put life into the running, then it is wisest to give it up for a day or two, and curtail the other exercise also. As regards food, most men can eat as much as they feel inclined, but one had better make a rule to take no liquid whatever between meals unless feeling unduly thirsty— as my old trainer (Nat Perry) used to say, " What you fancies you haves "—and it is no doubt wiser to quench one's thirst at any time than to go about with a dry and parched feeling in the mouth. The meat should be varied as much as possible, and poultry is a great aid in this direction ; toast is better to eat than bread, and all sorts of milk puddings with fruit, stewed or uncooked, according to the time of the year. The older an athlete is, the longer it takes him to get fit. I find myself that ten weeks of steady work is none too long ; moreover, it is advisable to allow a rather longer period than is absolutely necessary to guard against enforced rest through strains and other small ailments.

The last few days before an important race should be spent doing no hard work, but just trotting about the track to keep muscles well stretched. On the day of the race, a light and frugal meal should be partaken of some three hours at least before running ; the inside of a chop and one glass of port is quite sufficient for most men, and cannot be beaten.

Of opening medicines which are necessary to many men during hard work, three pills every Saturday night, and a seidlitz powder every Sunday morning, is the best possible aperient ; the part of the powder wrapped in blue paper should be placed in the glass of water overnight, so as to thoroughly dissolve. As Sunday should be a day of rest, any tiring effect of such medicine will have quite passed off before the next week's work commences. In conclusion, never worry because the running will not come after some weeks' training; remember that it cannot be forced in such a case, and increasing the work will often mean increasing in slowness; but if one faithfully works and waits, that state of complete fitness, as I must call it for want of a better term, is sure to follow.

CHAPTER III.

LEN HURST.

CHAMPION OF THE WORLD AT 20 MILES.

LEN HURST, the Long Distance Champion of the World, was born at Sittingbourne on the 28th December, 1871, is a brickmaker by trade, and scales, when in his best condition, about 10 stone 3 lbs. to 10 stone 5 lbs. He commenced his racing career in his native town in 1887, when he won a four miles' race and ran fourth in a ten miles' race.

The next year he came very quickly to the front, and experienced one of the most successful seasons ever achieved by an athlete. At the end of 1888, he was credited with no less than 31 first prizes in races from four to ten miles. Unfortunately, after so brilliant a record, business prevented him, during the seasons 1889-90 and 1891, from participating in a sport at which he had proved himself such an adept. Fortunately for the pedestrian world, he came back to the track in 1892, when his best performance was the 20 miles' race in which he defeated A. E. Ware, of Camden Town, to whom he conceded 440 yards, compelling his opponent to retire beaten at 11 miles. In 1893, he defeated Guy Temple, of Southwark, in a match at ten miles, the latter retiring when Hurst was three laps ahead. Later in the same year he performed the marvellous feat of running 183 miles in 30 hours, and subsequently pulled off four handicaps, three of four miles and one of six miles.

The season of 1894 was a quiet one, as nobody could be induced to try conclusions with him, but in December, 1895, he won a 20 hours' race at the Bethnal Green

LEN HURST.
Champion of the World 20 Miles and Upwards, World's Record Holder 16 and 17 Miles.

Excelsior Baths, totally eclipsing his previous long distance performances, covering 151 miles in the allotted time, a much better record than his previous one on the same track. In this competition he had the honour of defeating "Craig," of Inverness, or, as he is better known, George Blenner Hasset Tincler, the present day one, two, and three miles' champion of the world.

In the year 1896, finding business very quiet in this country, Hurst entered for the great 25 miles Marathon Race in France, the race being from Paris to Comflaus. There were 191 starters. Hurst won easily, in the fast time of 2 hours 31 minutes, beating all existing records, and securing, in addition to £40 first prize, £40 for breaking the record. The same year he easily defeated Mathlin, the French champion, and also comfortably disposed of Chovolot, another champion, to whom he conceded 880 yards in a race of 12½ miles.

In 1897 he met the celebrated runner Watkins, at Blackburn, in a 20 miles race for £200, and compelled him to retire at 15 miles. On being told he need go no further, Hurst surprised the spectators by sprinting another lap (quarter-of-a-mile) and throwing a somersault at the winning post.

In 1898, he met and defeated G. Crossland, holder of the 20 miles' record, in a race at ten miles for £200, Crossland retiring at six miles. Later in the same year, he again defeated Crossland over a similar distance. This same year he also met Bacon in a ten miles match at Ashton-under-Lyne, being beaten by a yard-and-a-half after a most exciting struggle, but he managed to get his revenge two or three weeks later by practically running Bacon to a standstill at Rochdale in a 15 miles match.

His next important match was in the early part of 1899, when he met and was defeated by Harry Watkins, of

Coventry, of whom it can safely be said that he is the finest four to 12 miles' runner the world has ever seen, this statement being backed up by the very easy manner in which he has recently knocked out not only the long standing one hour and ten miles records, but the recently-established record for one hour of F. E. Bacon.

Hurst's last match, before these notes go to press, was against Michael O'Neil, of Belfast, by whom he was defeated, after one of the most severe races (at five miles) seen for many a day. It would appear that Hurst has fallen on evil times, but when one comes to consider that the further he goes, the better he goes, and notices that for several years he has only had two matches in England over ten miles, one cannot be very much surprised; he would be delighted to meet any man in the world who will run him at 20 miles, when a substantial stake would be forthcoming.

Of this wonderful athlete it can be said that he is a steady, industrious, and conscientious man, who prides himself that he can undertake the task of running ten miles and making 8,000 bricks in 12 hours, and though, as above stated, he has been unsuccessful in his last two matches, he still lives and longs to fight another day.

Len Hurst has been good enough to add his ideas on training to those already set forth in this book.

CHAPTER IV.

Training Notes by Len Hurst.

In offering a few hints on distance running, I must crave the indulgence of my readers for the manner in which I may express myself, but as more of my time has been spent on the track than in school, an apology is hardly necessary.

In the first place, for a youth to attain anything like "class" honours, in events from ten miles and upwards, he must make up his mind that from the time he starts to practice, he will have two or three years' steady work ahead of him, and must be satisfied to plod along at what, to his ambitious mind, must appear a very slow pace. Experience teaches us that it is impossible for a man to possess both speed and endurance for long distance running without a thorough training.

I should, therefore, advise aspirants to this class of racing to take any amount of walking exercise, right from the time they start running, regulating their early spins to half-mile races only, against the day when they can do a creditable 20-mile performance.

Another good maxim for the distance man is "early to bed and early to rise," as by this practice a great reserve of energy is derived, and, to my way of thinking, a nice amount of work can be done, between rising and breakfast, in the way of quiet walks. For walking exercise, the early morning is the best part of the day, for in addition to the air being fresh and buoyant, this exercise creates a good appetite for breakfast, and is, therefore, a grand foundation for building the rest of the day's work on.

In the forenoon go down to your running quarters, and if the walk is not a long one, make up for that by negotiating about three miles round the track, after which strip and start at once to run at a moderate pace about half the distance of the race you have in view. Remember never to overdo yourself, or pump yourself quite out. On returning to your stripping box, indulge in a thorough grooming, taking care that the moisture on the body has been entirely dried, and that a pleasant glow exists, which will form a fair criterion that one is pretty well all right; and here I would impress the fact that these points must be well attended to, for unless the muscles are supple, no amount of practice will effect that pace, smoothness, and style so essential to success.

The morning's work having been carefully attended to, brings us to dinner time, a very material institution in the life of an athlete, and for this meal it is desirable that each man use his own discretion as to its composition. I would urge some especial care to be taken in its selection, and would suggest " ringing the changes " on the following :— Roast beef, roast and boiled mutton or chicken, helped out with a very limited amount of vegetable and bread; the latter ought to be " stale and crusty," and washed down with half-a-pint of good bitter ale. Half-an-hour's read, and then a full hour in bed, must follow this meal. On rising, have a nice rub down, and again set off to the track, where you indulge in work similar to that done in the forenoon, not forgetting, however, to have a little dash at the finish of your run, if you feel game. Another good grooming, which is about the last for the day, and a gentle stroll round before tea, a meal which should be quite plain. From 6.30 to 8.30 a good long walk, after which an " easy " till ten o'clock, when, after a biscuit or two, bed, and the healthy athlete will be quite ready for it.

This may appear a somewhat severe mode, but I do unhesitatingly assert that he who would succeed as a long distance runner will have to carefully train on these lines.

Having endeavoured to give a general outline to be adopted, it now rests with the man himself, and with his trainer, to add to or deduct any particulars that may not apply to the especial features in his case.

It is now, therefore, only left for me to briefly summarize a daily programme as follows :—Rise at six o'clock in summer and seven o'clock in winter ; cold sponge down ; steady walk ; 8.30, breakfast ; easy till 9.45 ; walk till 11 o'clock ; run about three miles ; dinner, 12.45 ; bed, 1.45 ; out for walk at three o'clock ; track at four ; three miles spin with sharp finish, shower and rub down ; tea, 5.30 ; walk, 6.30 to 8.30 ; quiet chat, read, or game of some sort ; and bed at ten o'clock. Never forget grooming on rising from bed at any time, and take sponge and shower baths cold.

CHAPTER V.

FRED. E. BACON.

THE CHAMPION OF THE WORLD AT ONE TO TEN MILES DURING 1895 TO 1898.

THE WORLD'S CHAMPION AT TEN MILES, 1899.

HOLDER OF THE WORLD'S RECORD FOR ONE HOUR (ELEVEN MILES, 1243 YARDS).

F. E. BACON was born at Boxted, Colchester, Essex, in November, 1870. His share of honours in the pedestrian world has been by no means small. As an amateur, he was a great handicap runner, his wins being too numerous to give in detail; but among his championships in those days might be mentioned the one mile in 1893, 1894, and 1895—the latter being one of the fastest miles he ever ran, namely, 4 min. 17 secs.—the four miles in 1894, and the ten miles in 1895. In the month of June, 1896, came the *fiat* of the A.A.A. that a number of champions and others must be suspended. Several of these men had been running with success in the professional ranks, both in handicaps and matches, and Bacon very judiciously joined issue with the professionals, so that from 1896 to his match with Watkins, at ten miles, on the 15th April, 1899, he was the accepted champion at that distance. In the meantime, on June 19th, 1897, he upset Deerfoot's record for one hour by covering 11 miles 1,243 yards; but, unfortunately, the championship for the shorter distances of one, two, and three miles, was taken from him in the month of May, 1897.

F. E. BACON.
The First Man to Beat Deerfoot's Long-Standing Record for One Hour by covering 11 miles, 1,243 yards.

In his teens he accepted the "Queen's Shilling," and spent a year or two soldiering, but finding he could run a bit, he purchased his discharge, so as to devote his energies to track work. And now that circumstances have compelled him to seek some other means of livelihood, he can be found in the very peaceful occupation of farming in the neighbourhood of his native village. When at his best, I can safely assert that there never lived a man who could finish as Bacon could in distance races, I myself having seen him at one, two, four, and ten miles finish the greater portion of the last lap with a dash and speed worthy of a sprinter.

Bacon's ideas on training are quite in accord with those of Bredin and Len Hurst, so that there is no need to specially state them at length.

CHAPTER VI.

GEORGE BLENNER-HASSET TINCLER.

G. B. TINCLER, the one, two, and three miles' champion of the World, first saw the light of day in the fine old Irish Capital, in the year 1874.

He commenced his career in his native city of Dublin, in 1892, his advent being a very auspicious one, as he defeated almost all comers, particularly in mile races. His talents, as an athlete, being so quickly demonstrated, it was natural that he should soon seek fresh worlds to conquer, and consequently he was very soon found further afield. The athletic world soon became aware of this, from the fact that he immediately appropriated the Irish Mile Championship, which he also won again the following year.

We next hear of him in connection with the great New Year's Carnival in Edinburgh, where, under the name of "Craig," he had the distinction of winning the great One Mile Handicap from scratch, a feat never before or since accomplished by any athlete.

During the seasons 1894 to 1897, Tincler raced with varying success, but in 1898 we find him firmly established among the best runners of the day. After a very considerable amount of finessing between his backers and those of Bacon, the then admitted world's champion at one to ten miles, a series of matches was arranged at one, two, and three miles, for £100 a side each match, and the title of World's Champion. The first of these races was the one mile, which took place on the splendid track of the Rochdale Athletic Society, and caused a tremendous amount of

Henderson, Photo.] [Rochdale.

G. B. TINCLER,
One, Two, and Three Mile Champion of the World.

excitement, both men running as though for a Kingdom. The subject of these lines performed so brilliantly, that at the finish he came home practically alone, in the very fine time of 4mins. 16⅔secs.; W. G. George's world's record time being 4mins. 12¾secs.

This performance proved to be no flash in the pan on his part, for in the second match, a very short time afterwards (May 21st), over two miles, he finished, going easily, in 9min. 19secs., and many experts were of opinion, that had he been "pushed" at all, the two miles record held since 1863, by old Bill Lang, would have been beaten. These performances, of course, established him as undisputed champion at these distances, and Bacon was so satisfied that he had at last met a better man than himself, that he paid forfeit for the third match at three miles. Tincler thus became, in the course of a couple of weeks, the World's Champion at one, two, and three miles, and one may here remark, that it will require a "great" man to depose him from his position.

His next important match was at half-mile, when he challenged E. C. Bredin, the long standing half-mile champion of the world, to a match to be run on the 18th February, 1899, and great was the excitement on that eventful day, each man knowing that every effort must be put forth, if victory was to result. Both men stripped as fit as the proverbial "Fiddle," and got away to a good start. Tincler commenced making the running, having at one stage as much as seven yards in hand; but Bredin, who is one of the finest judges of pace in the world, then began to close up the gap, and in a magnificent finish won, amidst a tremendous scene of excitement, by quarter-of-a-yard, time being 1min. 56⅕secs. This time has been beaten by nearly two seconds, but, as the race was run during the cold month of February, and not by any means under the most favourable conditions, the race must rank as one of the finest half-miles ever witnessed. Tincler next assayed to give Watkins 80 yards in two miles, on March 11th, but found the task much more than he bargained for. The Coventry runner, who had been going "great guns," and was, at the time, coming forward by leaps and bounds in the estimate of the public, simply won as he liked, Tincler being compelled to retire nearly half-a-mile from home.

In addition to the foregoing performances, Tincler has been very successful in America, where he holds the one and two miles' championship, and where, in 1897, he won 35 out of the 36 races he competed for. In 1898, he ran six races, and won them all, and this season, he has been again wonderfully successful, winning almost every event in which he competed.

Perhaps, no English winner is more popular in America, than Tincler. He has not yet attempted anything in the way of business or profession, other than his running, and thinks he will be fit for most men from a mark at his own distances, for some time to come. At the moment, he is very anxious to "try a throw," as the wrestlers say, with Cullum, the new half-mile champion, at that distance, or with Watkins at three miles, or will concede the latter 20 yards' start at two miles.

———>◁———

Photo by] [T. Andrew.
W. G. GEORGE,
Holder of the One Mile World's Record, 4mins. 12¾secs.

CHAPTER VII.

METHOD OF TRAINING IN THE EARLY PART OF THE PRESENT CENTURY.

SOME account of the manner in which a pedestrian was trained in the days before Her Majesty the Queen was born may, the Editor hopes, be found of interest to runners, both amateur and professional, boxing men, and athletes generally. The directions are those laid down by that celebrated pedestrian, Captain Barclay, perhaps best remembered as the man who, in the early part of the present century, walked 1,000 miles in 1,000 hours on Newmarket Heath. Captain Barclay came from a family celebrated for strength and athletic ability: his father was so powerful a man that it is narrated of him, that finding a stray horse in one of his fields he lifted it on his shoulders and threw it over the hedge; while his grandfather, when a member of Parliament, representing Kincardine, made it a practice to walk to Westminster, from Urie, his home, at the commencement of each session, and would pick up many a prize hat for cudgel play, and wrestling on the road. Our present members travel by express train at 50 miles an hour. "The times have changed for other things as well as training, and we with them." After reading the directions for training, it will be realized that the Captain, if he practised what he preached, had need, indeed, to be a strong man; such an awful course of purging and sweating were surely enough to reduce an ordinary individual to nothing better than a likely candidate for place honours in a coffin.

Think of starting on two ounces of Glauber's salts, to be followed by a similar dose four days after, and another four days after that. Then to get up every morning at five and do two hours of strong work before breakfast; and to continue day after day upon a diet consisting solely of beef, stale bread, and old ale.

In these old days there were some good men, though; I read in a newspaper of 1807 that on October 12th of that year, a foot race, for ten guineas, was run near Manchester between a cotton spinner and a hatter of that town, "when (to quote the paper), shameful to say, the former, being the best runner, was stopped at about a quarter of-a-mile after starting by a friend of the latter. The spinner, however, knocking down the intruder, fell over him, rose again, and actually beat his antagonist by upwards of 40 yards." The time for this race was returned as 4min.30sec. The name of the victor is, unfortunately, not recorded, but a man who could run a mile in 4min. 30sec., with a fight "thrown in" *en route*, must have been a champion.

Even in those days the matches made were sometimes subject to a suspicion of having been arranged. In 1807 one, Abraham Wood, made a match with Captain Barclay, before mentioned; Wood to go as he pleased and Barclay to walk for 24 hours, Wood to give 20 miles start. The match was for 600 guineas. Wood went 40 miles in six hours, having then gained four miles upon Barclay, who did 36 miles. Then Wood stopped, and when the paper from which we take the account went to press, the dispute as to the payment or non-payment of bets was still raging. How they settled we cannot tell, further intelligence being wanting.

Tom Cribb was trained by Captain Barclay for his fight with Molineaux for the championship, which took place on

Ratcliffe, Photo.] [Southport.

W. SANDERTON, "TREACLE,"

A Champion, One to Three Miles, in the Early Sixties, whose great struggles with Bill Lang are so remembered by the old school.

the 29th September, 1811. Cribb arrived at Urie to commence training on the 7th July, and, to quote a contemporary record, "he then weighed 16 stone, and from his mode of living in London, and the confinement of a crowded city, he had become corpulent, big bellied, full of gross humours, and short-breathed, and it was with difficulty he could walk ten miles."

Before the end of August Cribb's weight was reduced to 13st. 5lbs., which was found to be pitch of condition. We may conclude from this that one "Thomas Cribb was put through the mill" in no half-hearted fashion; but that he was put into the ring in fine condition there can be no possible doubt.

The great fault with old-time trainers would appear to be that they went in for too much "training," and not enough practice; no amount of sweating will improve a man without the practice.

The art of training for athletic exercises consists of purifying the body and strengthening its powers by certain processes, which thus qualify a person for laborious exertions. It was known to the ancients, who paid much attention to the means of augmenting corporeal vigour and activity and, accordingly, among the Greeks and Romans, certain rules of regimen and exercise were prescribed to the candidates for gymnastic celebrity.

The great object of training for running or boxing matches is to increase the muscular strength, and to improve the free action of the lungs, or wind, of the person subjected to the process, which is done by medicines, regimen, and exercise. That these objects can be accomplished is evident from the nature of the human system. It is well known (for it has been demonstrated by experiments) that every part of the firmest bones is successively absorbed and deposited. The bones and their ligaments, the muscles and their tendons—all the finer and all the more flexible parts of the body—are as properly a secretion, as the saliva that flows from the mouth, or the moisture that bedews the surface. The health of all the parts, and their soundness of structure, depends upon this perpetual absorption and perpetual renovation ; and exercise, by promoting at once absorption and secretion, promotes life without hurrying it, renovates all the parts, and preserves them apt and fit for every office. When the human frame is thus capable of being altered and renovated, it is not surprising that the art of training should be carried to a degree of perfection almost incredible ; and that by certain processes the breath, strength, and courage of man should be so greatly improved as to enable him to perform the most laborious undertakings. That such effects have been produced is unquestionable, being fully exemplified in the astonishing exploits of our most celebrated pedestrians, which are the infallible results of preparatory discipline. The skilful trainer attends to the state of the bowels, the lungs, and the skin ; and he uses such means as will reduce the fat, and, at the same time, invigorate the muscular fibres. The patient is purged by drastic medicines; he is sweated by walking under a weight of clothes, and by lying between feather beds ; his limbs are roughly rubbed ; his diet is beef or mutton ; his drink strong ale ; and he is gradually inured to exercise by repeated trials in walking and running. By attenuating the fat, emptying the cellular substance, hardening the muscular fibre, and improving the breath, a man of the ordinary frame may be made to fight for one hour with the utmost exertion of strength and courage, or to go over 100 miles in 24 hours.

The most effectual process for training is that practised by Captain Barclay, and the particular mode which he has

Gregson, Photo.] [Blackpool.

W. CUMMINGS,
Holder of the Ten Miles' Record, September, 1885, to September, 1899.

adopted has not only been sanctioned by professional men, but has met with the unqualified approbation of amateurs. The following statement, therefore, contains the most approved rules, and is presented to the reader as the result of much experience, founded on the theoretic principles of the art.

The pedestrian, who may be supposed in tolerable condition, enters upon his training with a regular course of physic, which consists of three doses. Glauber's salts are generally preferred, and from one ounce and a half to two ounces are taken each time, with an interval of four days between each dose. After having gone through the course of physic, he commences regular exercise, which is gradually increased as he proceeds in the training. When the object in view is to accomplish a pedestrian match, his regular exercise may be from 24 miles a day. He must rise at five in the morning, run half a-mile at the top of his speed up hill, and then walk six miles at a moderate pace, coming in about seven to breakfast, which should consist of beef-steak or mutton chop, under-done, with stale bread and old beer. After breakfast he must again walk six miles at a moderate pace, and at twelve lie down in bed without his clothes for half-an-hour. On getting up he must walk four miles, and return by four to dinner, which should also be beef-steaks or mutton chops, with bread and beer as at breakfast. Immediately after dinner he must resume his exercise by running half-a-mile at the top of his speed, and walking six miles at a moderate pace. He takes no more exercise for that day, but retires to bed about eight, and next morning proceeds in the same manner.

CHAPTER VIII.

METHOD OF TRAINING, ETC. (*Continued*).

AFTER having gone in this regular course for three or four weeks, the pedestrian must take a four mile sweat, which is produced by running four miles in flannel, at the top of his speed. Immediately on returning, a hot liquor, of which he must drink one English pint, is prescribed, in order to promote the perspiration. It is termed the sweating liquor, and is composed of the following ingredients, viz., one ounce of carraway seed, half-an-ounce of coriander seed, an ounce of root liquorice, and half-an-ounce of sugar candy, mixed with two bottles of cider, and boiled down to one-half. He is then put to bed in his flannels, and being covered with six or eight pairs of blankets, and a feather bed, must remain in this state from 25 to 30 minutes, when he is to be taken out and rubbed perfectly dry. Being then well wrapped in a great-coat, he walks out gently for two miles to breakfast, which, on such occasions, should consist of a roasted fowl. He afterwards proceeds with his usual exercise. These sweats are continued weekly, till within a few days of the performance of the match, or in other words, he must undergo three or four of these operations. If the stomach of the pedestrian be foul, an emetic or two must be given about a week before the conclusion of the training, and he is now supposed to be in the highest condition. Besides his usual or regular exercise, a person under training ought to employ himself, in the intervals, in every kind of exertion which tends to activity, such as cricket, bowls, throwing quoits, etc., that during the whole day both body and mind may be constantly occupied.

The diet or regimen is the next point of consideration, and is very simple. As the intention of the trainer is to preserve the strength of the pedestrian, he must take care to keep him in good condition by nourishing food. Animal diet is alone prescribed, and beef and mutton are preferred. The lean of fat beef cooked in steaks, with very little salt, is the best, and it should be rather under-done than otherwise. Mutton being reckoned easy of digestion, may be occasionally given, to vary the diet and gratify the taste. The legs of the fowl are highly esteemed. It is preferable to have the meat broiled, as much of its nutritive quality is lost by roasting or boiling. Biscuit and stale bread are the only preparations of vegetable matter which are permitted to be given, and everything inducing flatulency must be carefully avoided. Veal and lamb are never allowed, nor pork, which operates as a laxative on some people ; all fat or greasy substances are prohibited, as they induce bile, and consequently injure the stomach. But it has been proved by experience, that the lean of meat contains more nourishment than the fat, and in every case the most substantial food is preferable to any other kind.

Vegetables, such as turnips, carrots, or potatoes, are never given, as they are watery and of difficult digestion. On the same principle, fish must be avoided, and, besides, it is not sufficiently nutritious. Neither butter nor cheese is allowed ; the one being very indigestible, and the other apt to turn rancid on the stomach. Eggs are also forbidden, excepting the yolk taken raw in the morning. And it must be remarked, that salt, spices, and all kinds of seasonings, with the exception of vinegar, are prohibited.

With respect to liquors, they must always be taken cold ; and home brewed beer, old but not bottled, is the best. A little red wine, however, may be given to those who are not fond of malt liquor, but never more than half-a-pint after dinner. Too much liquor swells the abdomen, and, of course, injures the breath. The quantity of beer, therefore, should not exceed three pints during the whole day, and it must be taken with breakfast and dinner, no supper being allowed.

Water is never given alone, and ardent spirits are strictly prohibited, however diluted. It is an established rule to avoid liquids as much as possible, and no more liquor of any kind is allowed to be taken than what is merely requisite to quench the thirst. Milk is never allowed, as it curdles on the stomach. Soups are not used; nor is anything liquid taken warm, but gruel or broth, to promote the operation of the physic, and the sweating liquor mentioned above. The broth must be cooled in order to take off the fat, when it may be again warmed, or beef tea may be used in the same manner, with little or no salt. In the days between the purges, the pedestrian must be fed as usual, strictly adhering to the nourishing diet, by which he is invigorated.

Profuse sweating is resorted to as an expedient for removing the superfluities of flesh and fat. Three or four sweats are generally requisite, and they may be considered the severest part of the process.

Emetics are only prescribed if the stomach be disordered, which may sometimes happen, when due care is not taken to proportion the quantity of food to the digestive powers; but in general, the quantity of aliment is not limited by the trainer, but left entirely to the discretion of the pedestrian, whose appetite should regulate him in this respect. Although the chief parts of the training system depend upon sweating, exercise, and feeding, yet the object to be obtained by the pedestrian would be defeated if they were not adjusted to each other, and to his constitution. The skilful trainer will, therefore, constantly study the progress of his art, by observing the effects of the processes separately, and in combination.

It is impossible to fix a precise period from the completion of the training process, as it depends upon the condition of the pedestrian; but from two to three months, in most cases, will be sufficient, especially if he be in tolerable condition at the commencement, and possessed of sufficient perseverance and courage to submit cheerfully to the privations and hardships to which he must unavoidably be subjected.

The criterion by which it may be known whether a man be in good condition, or, what is the same thing, properly trained, is the state of the skin, which becomes smooth, elastic, and well coloured, or transparent. The flesh is also firm, and the person trained feels himself light and full of spirits. But in the progress of the training, his condition may be as well ascertained by the effect of the sweats, which cease to reduce his weight, and by the manner in which he performs one mile at the top of his speed, as to walk a hundred; and, therefore, if he performs this short distance well, it may be concluded that his condition is perfect, or that he has derived all the advantages which can possibly result from the training process.

CHAPTER IX.

TRAINING FOR BOYS.

(*By Cantab.*)

EVERY school, nowadays, has its athletic sports, and the boy who wishes to shine in these contests should begin to train at least a month beforehand. Schoolboys should be more or less fit all the year round, even in the summer holidays, when cricket does not impose restrictions as to the number of ices, etc., eaten between meals, and loafing is the order of the day. Any boy who trains carefully for the school sports, between the ages of 12 and 16, will reap the benefit of it in after years. He should be very careful not to strain himself, or to do too much, for he must remember that he is growing all the time; his limbs and body are not fully developed, and all training, until the body is fully grown, should be looked upon year by year as a gradual preparation for something better to come. Before we begin talking of the work itself, let us chat for a moment on the question of diet. Do not eat between meals, and do not drink more than half-a-pint of milk, water, or cocoa at each meal. I consider these three liquids the best drinks for a boy to train on. The boy who drinks anything in the way of alcohol, or smokes, is simply handicapping himself for the present and the future. Although this book has been entirely confined to pedestrians, I have the editor's permission to include in this article a few hints on the other branches of athletic sports. Running we will, naturally, deal with first, and, at any rate to begin with, for boys, I do not believe in any attempt to train being made before

Burchill, Photo.] [Bristol.
H. CULLUM,
Welsh Champion. Recently defeated E. C. Bredin for Half-mile World's Championship.

breakfast. In the summer a swim does no harm first thing in the morning, provided a biscuit is eaten directly you get up. During the winter months a sharp walk for five or ten minutes is the best beginning one can make for the day. The real work of the day should be done before the mid-day meal, and about five or six in the evening, if possible just before tea time. If you have the time and the opportunity, do not forget that a cold sponge or a shower bath is a capital thing after your work. It is as well to dispense with the ordinary school games during your period of training.

On the question of clothes there is not very much to be said. A thin running vest without sleeves, thin satin knickers, and a good thick sweater high in the neck and with plenty of room in it, are the only essentials.

In the matter of shoes, spikes, of course, are the best, although a boy should not be too eager to don them until he has become fairly proficient in starting, sprinting, etc. When you do invest in a pair of running shoes see that the spikes are not too long, that the leather is nice and soft, and that it fits the foot, over a wash-leather sock, like a glove. Directly you get on to the track or into the field which you have selected as a training ground, do a jog trot over about a quarter-of-a-mile, finishing the last 20 yards with a fair sprint, to stretch your legs and open your lungs. Then, in view of the sprinting races, get someone to practise you in getting sharply away from your mark. Unless a boy is a Downer, the best position for a good start, to my mind, is the following :—

Have your left foot toeing the line, knee bent, body, head, and arms reaching slightly forward. Your right leg should be far enough back to keep the balance even. In this way most of the weight should be thrown on the toes, in such a manner that one is ready to spring forward the moment the word is given. Once started, never look behind you under any circumstances. A race is never won until the tape is breasted, and always remember to finish every race as if you had not an inch of ground to give away.

From the very first, except in races under 150 yards, where you will have to go your hardest all the time, try and cultivate judgment in your running, use your head as well as your feet, get to know your own powers and possibilities beforehand, do not leave them to be found out on the day of the race. For instance, if you find the pace on starting too fast and furious, hang back a little, and keep something in hand for the finish. Many of your too sanguine competitors are sure to suffer for forcing the pace, and remember, as I said before, that a race is never entirely lost until one, two, and three have breasted the tape, and the last man often finds himself leading at the conclusion of the race. As far as possible, try and breathe through your nose when running; and it will not be out of place, while chatting about breathing, to give you an exercise which you can practise for the development of your lung capacity. Lie flat on your back, feet together, with the arms extended and placed flat against your sides. Slowly raise your arms, keeping them all the time quite stiff, until your hands are touching the floor at the back of your head. As the arms go backward, inhale through your nose, until the lungs are inflated to their utmost capacity; even when they seem full, try and sniff in a small extra quantity; you will generally find room for it. When the lungs are fully inflated, slowly bring the arms back to their original position, exhaling the air briskly through the mouth.

In training for sprinting races, never at first run quite up to your full speed—that is to say, do not strain yourself at the finish if there is not plenty left in you. You will improve slowly when you have been at it a few days. About a couple of sprints over the whole distance at one time, with rest in between, should be quite enough, and then, perhaps, a jog trot of about a couple of miles to build up your power of endurance. Long sharp walks are a great help, especially for races of half-a-mile and upwards, and occasional sprints along the walk will give variety to the expedition. I would advise every boy, when he runs, to hold a pair of corks or a couple of pieces of wood. I have always found it great comfort to have something to grip when you are making your final effort. Get on the track, when possible, twice a day, with an interval of, at least, four hours in between. So much for running. Now for a word as to the high jump.

A capital exercise to improve the springing powers of the legs is the skipping rope, and also walking on the tips of your toes with the hands locked on the back of the head. One very important point in connection with high jumping is to take off from the proper place. One of the best tests as to whether one is doing so, is to stand on your left leg a small distance from the bar, and raise the right so that the tip of the toe just touches the bar. When this can be done, with the right leg perfectly rigid and at right angles to the left, the spot on which the left leg stands should be the point from which to take off.

Beware of too long a run. Twelve or fourteen feet should be quite enough, and take care not to rush at your jumps like a bull at a gate, but approach them with a quick, springy step. As you rise from the ground, gather up your legs underneath you or at your side, and take care not to strike the bar with your hands; many a fine jump has been spoilt in this way.

With regard to the question of the long jump, one cannot get up too much pace before the take off, and plenty of space should be allowed for the run, to enable the jumper to spring when he is at the top of his speed. Remember to bring your feet well forward, stretching out your head and arms, so that, after landing in the "batter," you do not fall back into a sitting position, and get disqualified.

Putting the shot is now general in most schools for boys over 14, and any boy who will go in for one or two simple dumb-bell exercises will be able to add several inches to his present putting form.

It is a mistake to think that lifting heavy weights, or using heavy dumb-bells, helps one in putting the shot. Of course, strength, weight, and height are of great importance, but there is also a good deal in the knack of putting.

Perhaps the best style to adopt in putting the weight is as follows:—Balance yourself on the right foot with the weight lying in the palm of your right hand, lower the body slightly, and lean a little back. Then commence swinging your left leg once or twice to get up the impetus; then, taking a hop with your right foot, still keeping your body slightly lowered, swing your left foot forward and plant it on the line as near the mark as possible. As you place your left foot on the line, shoot the weight away from you as smartly as possible, bringing your body to its full height, in this way getting the full advantage of all your inches and weight. Be very careful, however, not to let any part of your shoe overstep the mark, as this will disqualify your put.

Tug-of-war and throwing the hammer need not concern us here, but we will conclude this article with a few hints on hurdling.

Very few boys can hope to be first-class hurdlers without a great deal of practice, and it is folly for a boy to compete in any hurdle races until he has learned to fly his hurdles properly. Ordinary jumping is not the thing, and only causes loss of time between the sticks.

Let the tyro begin from the very first trying to fly his hurdles—that is, to skim over the hurdles, drawing one of your legs behind you. In this way you land on one foot, with the other ready at once to take the forward stride. Men like Paget Tomlinson take three strides between their hurdles, but for a boy certainly the correct number is five. Every care should be taken to get a good start, and the fly over the first hurdle should be constantly practised. Do not get flurried, even if you are pushed a little. It is much better to take your hurdles in your stride. If you get flurried and lose your stride, you are bound to come to grief.

———>·<———

www.ingramcontent.com/pod-product-compliance
Lightning Source LLC
Chambersburg PA
CBHW070155100426
42743CB00013B/2923